SUSPENDED SENTENCE

The Lynching

by
Benjamin S. Bradford

BENJAMIN S. BRADFORD
23101 HARDING ST.
HAZEL PARK, MI 48030

Table of Contents

CAROL –

BEST WISHES – HOPE

YOU ENJOY!

Benjamin S. Bradford

9-5-01

SUSPENDED SENTENCE

Charles J. Humphries passed away in 1994, without seeing the results of our efforts, his as well as mine, in this research. He was a treasure to find, a great source of information and support! This picture was taken at the Evans Cemetery by Ben Bradford in May, 1993.

The Lynching of William Monroe and John Evans

Between ten o'clock and midnight on 15 August 1891, two men died under circumstances that still leave some people wondering. The circumstances were such that many people felt that they were justified in taking these lives, even though they were taken from the hands of the law and summarily hanged!

A hue and cry went up from everyone in high places, including the Honorable Thomas Jones, governor of Alabama, to bring the perpetrators to justice, while a very substantial ratio of the population felt they had left justice hanging on a tree about half a mile from Baileyton, Alabama, on that fateful night!

As to whether what happened that night was right, that is what the debate is still about! As to whether the men deserved to die by the hands of a mob, I cannot say, but apparently the wheels of justice in our legal and judicial system were grinding out something besides justice, or those people would much sooner have felt it's bite!

This story, while observing the facts where available, is intended to fill the gaps in the previous versions of this story, with the best logic available to the author where the facts are not known. It is difficult, as it involved the best cover-up of which the citizenry of the area were capable. The incentives? The leading citizens of the area were involved, not a bunch of itinerant bums. The crime of murder carries no statute of limitations, if one of them could be found today, alive after more than a hundred years, with sufficient evidence they could still legally be brought to trial!

Some of the crimes and offenses commonly attributed to William Monroe Evans and his son John Henry Evans are outlined herein. Most of the evidence had to come from outside Cullman County, initially. The cover-up placed upon the facts of this case was not known even to people such as my mother, who grew up in the immediate community where the Evanses lived, died, and were buried, she being born in 1896, only one year after the trial.

The newspaper accounts kept in the archives were sometimes a bitter disappointment, as key articles I was looking for had been "surgically removed" by previous researchers, rather than write them down in longhand, as they didn't have photographic copiers available to them. Could this destruction of recorded information have been part of the cover-up?

The court records were difficult to get at, with some still available in Cullman County, but with most of them residing elsewhere, such as probably the Federal Court records in Atlanta, Georgia, (Ku Klux Klan related) or quite possibly simply "trashed". This left me with the folklore approach along with many other sources, such as second-hand or third-hand eyewitnesses of some events.

The old baptizin' hole and swimmin' hole at Welcome Falls is my old stomping grounds as a boy. This is the source of one of the related stories, the old foot-peddler whose skeletal remains were found on the ledge under the falls. He was believed to be a murder victim of the Evans duo.

Also included in this work, you will find a short story dealing with the peddler by Joan Mims, written from the viewpoint of a psychic. She is an Evans relative as well as a Bradford relative. The cover of this book is her work, also. Thanks a lot, Joan!

I am deeply indebted to many people, especially Margaret Jean Jones, who was a tremendous help with information from her own research, Martha Belle (Holcomb) Davis, who has an excellent memory and a lot of knowledge, Betty Taylor, who helped very much with the cornerstone work, in other words, getting started! Carolina Nigg and Charles Rice were very helpful, too!

And then there's Charles J. Humphries, a treasured friend who is no longer with us. He passed away in early 1994. Charles was a man who paid attention to the older people, as evidenced by the video-taped interview I had with him. I asked him if the crime wave of which the pair were accused stopped when they died, and his answer was "The community became 'God's little acre' after the lynching!"

Lila Mabel (Holmes) Burks, niece of John S. and James Huston Holmes, was extremely helpful, telling me about actual conversations she had with them and others before my time. Unfortunately, she passed away December 12, 1996, at age 93, leaving me with many treasured memories!

Ora (Keller) Holmes was very helpful with information that wasn't available from any other source. She was born August 21, 1897, and there aren't too many people available whose experience goes that deep!

She was the daughter of Dr. Louis Montiville

4

Benjamin S. Bradford, with Lila Mabel (Holmes) Burks, who was a niece of John S. Holmes and James Huston Holmes. She was the daughter of their brother, A.M.B. Holmes. Mabel passed away December 12, 1996. She was a lovely lady!

Keller. She furnished me with a picture of Dr. Keller and answered many questions for me about people of that time and place. Miss Ora, Thanks from the bottom of my heart! I am also looking forward to attending that hundredth birthday party in this year, 1997 if at all possible. I have never attended one before!

The follow-up to the known information from the past is the actual trial. Everyone with whom I had talked with in the past was sure that no one was ever accused or went to trial. It took a lot of poking and

Ora with some of her favorite children and husband Archie Bethel Holmes.

searching to even find the "raveling thread" to pull on to get into the actual facts of the matter.

I am including, in several cases the actual documents, copied from the actual newspaper accounts as well as the actual hand-written court records. While at times they might be a little tedious, I feel it is beyond my level of expertise to edit them, they seem to tell the story rather well in their own right.

I am including a "cast of characters", or participants, which is somewhat statistical in one way, but you will probably be as surprised to find your relatives there as I was to find mine! They include some of such people as judge, jury, attorneys, defendants, and other participants, including bondsmen, and even some relatives, such as spouses thereof.

I will also attempt to document some of the crimes and offenses perpetrated by William Monroe Evans, although there are many I cannot find, and the information is sketchy on the ones I did find. My heartfelt thanks to many others, too numerous to mention here, but without whose help this book would have been impossible!

Any apparent bias is due to the availability of information, with some people just being better known than others. Sorry for the diversity, I tried!

I am sure there are errors in my research, but I feel it is the best effort ever made to understand this historic event, I did the best of which I am capable, I ask your forgiveness for error, and I sincerely hope you enjoy reading this as much as I have enjoyed writing it!

Benjamin S. Bradford.

Suspended Sentence Chapter One

In the beginning

In the year of 1845 a happy event took place in the Honeycomb Creek (Cottonville) area of Marshall County, Alabama. The occasion was the birth of a child who would be known as William Monroe Evans, later called "Mun", but had they been able to see his bizarre date with destiny as it would unfold the day might have been a little less happy.

The joyful parents were William Evans, who was 51 years old at the time, and his wife Mary, 37. I don't know for sure, but this looks like a second marriage for William. Children at that time were Mary M. Evans, 7 (probably the only child by the first marriage) John H. Evans, 1, (who was with William Monroe at the incident at Wild Goat Cove, probably the namesake for the son who would later join William Monroe in infamy), and William Monroe "Mun" Evans, to come one year after John H. Three years later came another daughter, Mary E. Evans (another indication of a second marriage, two daughters named Mary!) and two years after that would come Benjamin F. Evans, who would later attain some infamy from and with his brother "Mun".

Little is known about William Monroe Evans during the several following years, except for references made to that period later by people who wrote about him, with very little that could be called specific. Apparently he made it through to about seventeen or eighteen before getting into serious trouble. Education evidently wasn't his long suit, as he was signing paperwork shortly before his untimely demise with an "X".

At the same time William Monroe "Mun" was being born, another who would figure prominently into his future was already a lad of 16, and was already proving to be less than an asset to his community. In his lifetime he would rival even the notorious Ben Harris, known for the infamous Buck Island massacre in the Tennessee River, for the title of "Most hated man in this part of the country during the Civil War!"

We will pick him up in the 1850 census of Madison County, Alabama, in the broadly general area where Mun Evans was born. His name is John W. Dickey, (1829/1903?), his wife is Celina, maiden name unknown, but suspected by the author to be Evans. Both are 22, and have one child, Mary E, who is nine months old. Dickey is a sharp contrast to William Monroe Evans, in that he seems to be rather well educated for that time and place, leaving behind a hand-written scouting report and a payroll voucher with the United States Army, among other things.

This family reappears in the 1860 census (bear in mind this is immediately before the Civil War, which started in 1861) with both John and Celina at 31, and Mary E. (Elizabeth, for Grandma Evans?) is 10, and they have added Margaret, who is 8, David at 4, Alexander G. is 3, and Emily J. is 8 mos. John is listed as a farmer.

Next door we find Elizabeth Evans, 54, who was born in Georgia. She has children Milton H. at 19, Frances L. (female) at 17, and Richard M. at 15. Celina would fit into this family nicely! I have noticed a pronounced and continuing association between the Evans and Dickey families, leading me to believe there was intermarriage between the two families. Elizabeth might well have been his mother-in-law.

The preceding becomes suspect, though, when one interviews Jack Dickey, grandson of John *(C)*. Dickey as I did on Monday, 27 Jan 1997. I also talked with Holly Pritchett, John's grand son-in-law, who remembered Mrs. John Dickey as "Aunt Tommie", whose maiden name was Harless. His memory is reinforced by the fact that she was the first dead person he had ever seen in his young life. Both John and wife rest in the New Hope Cemetery, New Hope, Alabama.

Jack still lives on the original Dickey home site at New Hope. Jack's father was Walter Bell Dickey. Walter doesn't appear on any of these census reports, as he wasn't born until 1878. However, note the other children follow through except for spelling errors from one census to another!

There is the very real possibility of two (or even more) wives for John W. Dickey, which could easily make both of these stories true!

I am surprised to find that John Dickey and family are still around in 1870, despite Nabors'

saying he had gone "West". The entry is as follows:
U.S. Census (1870) Alabama

Kennamer P. O. , Marshall County, recorded
June 1, 1870

#40/40 John Dickey 40 tanner $6000/1000 b
Alabama

Seliney	42	Born Al.
		"
Elinor	20	"
Margaret	17	"
David	13	"
Alex	11	"
Emily	9	"
James	6	"
Lydia	4	"
Laura	1	"

(Same house)

Catherine Neal	45	keeping house
Claxton Marshal	24	farm laborer

John Kennamer was #50/50 in this census, placing him ten doors away from the Dickey family.
He, too, was a "Yankee" in the Civil War, probably the beginning of his acquaintance with John W. Dickey.

To conclude these interviews, I was told that John Dickey "died in the woods", in some kind of logging accident, that might have been interpreted as something other than an accident, and which might even have been the past reaching out for him with retribution in the form of murder!

The family believes John Dickey went to Texas for a while, as per the letter of A.M. Nabors, but if this happened it would have had to be for less than ten years, as he was always in Alabama for the census, occurring every ten years! As I learn more about the situation, I become more inclined to doubt that he ever went "West", as Nabors said!

There is one fly in the ointment, however! On the tombstone of the John Dickey, buried in New Hope Cemetery, he is identified as John <u>C</u>. Dickey! This might very well make him the John C. Dickey mentioned in the letter asking for Federal troops to restore peace in that area. They were most likely related, but I am unable to say *how* they were related at the present time!

In 1891 A.M. Nabors would write a letter to the editor of some newspapers, entitled "Monroe Evans, a True History of his Life and Character". This letter gives us a lot of the information available on either John Dickey or Mun Evans at that period of their lives. We will deal with said letter later, when it will become appropriate.

Very little that is good is said about either of the two above mentioned individuals, and as we progress it becomes easier to understand why.

With the advent of the Civil War a whole new field of opportunity opened up for John W. Dickey. He is reported by Nabors to have hated his neighbors, and to have treated his family shamefully as a matter of routine.

When he became aware that Union forces were

occupying the North shore of the Tennessee River in 1863, he made his move by going to the command-ing officer of those forces and impressing upon him that he was such a loyal Unionist that it was to the Commander's advantage to authorize an irregular scout company, to be selected, enlisted, and com-manded by himself, John Dickey. It seems a little strange, but the commander took him at his word, and did so authorize. The information indicates that the commander of Federal forces who appointed him directed Col. W.P. Lyon to do so, through an order from C.A. Defas(?) to the effect that the Com-manding General directed that John Dickey be hired at $3.00 per day as a scout., order dated Oct. 3, 1864.

Report by John Dickey, Federal Scout
Report:

I left Chattanooga on the 16th Oct and according to instructions received from Capt. Snodgraf, Comd'ing Scouts proceeded up the Tennessee River on the other side to a point within four miles of the Hiwasse River. I reached there on Tuesday, 20th March. I stopped at the house of a Mr. Peirsons, on the night of the 21st two men of Genl. Spears' Brig. crossed the river to see their family. They returned the same night and reported that the Rebel Cavalry had been moving up the river on the 20th and 21st and had crossed the Hiwasse River. They also re-ported that there were 300 Rebel Infantry at George-town.

The general report among the citizens is that the Federal troops are at Cleveland and that the cars are running to that point. I heard the whistle of the locomotive in that direction.

The three Reg'ts. that were stationed on this side of the river-two miles above Dallas had moved from there about five days since but they did not know to what place.

The citizens say that all the tents on this side of the river-near Edwards Island disappeared four or five days ago.

(signed)
John Dickey

With this kind of mandate, Dickey being hired by the Federal Government, began a reign of terror along the Tennessee River in six counties, Madison, Marshall, Jackson, Morgan, Limestone, and Lawrence. Under the cover of his claim of Federal loyalty, John Dickey recruited the most bizarre collection of depraved humanity ever seen in that part of the country. They were composed of known outlaws, Confederate deserters, traitors to the Union, conscription dodgers, and other riffraff that quickly was attracted by the thrills and profits of such a gang. I feel it is rather safe to say that more than one Evans brother was in this scout company, as well, probably including Benjamin F. and John H. Evans. They showed up in rather close association with William Monroe Evans on some of his escapades in later years!

One recruit to this menagerie for sure was, you guessed it, William Monroe Evans! He was at about the age of 18 at the time of his enlistment, or simply becoming one of the Dickey scout group without formality, in 1863. I suppose the things he was to experience during the next year or so would have destroyed the moral values of far more stable minds that Mun's.

The group so organized went forth to perform it's destiny, which was to rob, rape, murder, loot, and pillage! It is reported that many men, including the elderly and otherwise disabled, were dragged from their homes and executed before the eyes of their families by this gang, or army unit, if you prefer. Often on their raids the home was ignited, and the women, after being abused to the pleasures of this gang, were left without food or shelter for their children as well as themselves. This harsh treatment was imposed for no greater reason or excuse than that their husband, father, brother, son, etc. was in or sympathetic with the Confederate army, coupled with greed and lust on the part of the so-called scouts.

It was reported by some that the Dickey scout company was benevolent where the women were concerned, but that doesn't hold up under a good light. Even to credit him with morals in that category is hard to believe with him burning homes and casting mothers with children out in the winter weather without food or shelter.

Brutality of this type had to contribute a bit to the

moral degradation of William Monroe Evans in his formative years. Probably there has never been a youth who could go through such an experience and then get back on the straight and narrow.

Many people died at the hands of this gang, a few were listed in Nabors' material. One that he mentioned was Volney Ellett. I have found that the property where Trinity Methodist Church stood, on the road between Decatur and Moulton, Alabama, was donated by William Ellett and his wife in the 1830's, and the Church was burned to the ground by Federal forces during the Civil War. This leads me to believe that Volney's death was connected in some unknown way to that Church.

John Knox, in "A History of Morgan County, Alabama", tells us about some of the atrocities committed in that campaign.

Other names mentioned in connection with the depredations were Alfred Clark, Davis Russell, and Fletcher Lewis. Nabors refers to them as "fell by their hands."

Davis "Doc" Russell perished in the incident of the "Hewed log barn", at the hands of what Charles Rice describes in his excellent book "Hard Times" as "Home-made Yankees", of the stripe of Dickey and Evans. They were very likely the men of Dickey and Evans, without Dickey and Evans, as they were captured at the scene. The old barn stood at the Perkins place, on the Belle Fonte road North of Grant, Alabama. He was shot and fatally wounded by a picket (sentinel) from inside the barn. He was carried away from the scene on a litter, dying later. Russell family tradition recalls that he was killed at a log barn in Marshall County while serving with the unit of Milus Johnston known as the "Bushwhackers" in late 1864. This unusual "irregular" scout company was created for the purpose of scouting for, and actually piloting the Federal forces in their activities around the Tennessee Valley. Their regular range, with some exceptions, was roughly from Huntsville, Guntersville, Lacy's Spring, somewhere in that area, to over past Decatur, to the Moulton area. Can you imagine the opportunity for spoils such a circuit would have afforded to a gang of ambitious riffraff such as that?

I found it surprising that Federal forces were active in the Tennessee Valley from 1863, near the opening of the Civil War (1861/1865), but many cities and other locations along the Tennessee River, such as river ferries and boat landings, changed hands fairly often during most of the Civil War. It seems Federal forces had the power to take them, but not the manpower to occupy and hold them, as a general rule.

The fighting in this area could not very well be described as conventional warfare, as atrocities by each side tended to result in escalation by the other side, until it became the scene of several atrocities and reprisals. Per John Knox, in his "A History of Morgan County, Alabama", some Federal officers were more interested in capturing cotton bales than Rebels. It seems both sides were self serving soldiers of fortune, rather than loyal to their respective causes.

While Mun wasn't necessarily the brains or leadership of this scout unit, he remained with Dickey throughout it's lifetime in the war, from the winter of 1863 through most of 1864, and didn't even leave the country, as John Dickey was *reported* to do by Nabors, *although perhaps he didn't*! The Dickey family shows up in the 1870 census located in Kennamer Cove, near Grant, North of Guntersville, Alabama, as previously mentioned.

I had looked for Dickey in the Oklahoma and Missouri area, as I thought he might have gone there to join up with Quantrill and his Commancheros after the war, due to the similarity of their operating styles, but apparently he was rather quiet in Alabama, neither creating nor inviting too much publicity. While I haven't investigated him beyond this point in this era, I haven't heard of any crime wave he created, either.

William Monroe Evans continued to live on in the Honeycomb Creek area near Guntersville, Alabama, in Marshall County, and continued to exploit the country in a similar manner to what he had done before, but broadening his range of criminal activity over a much wider section of Alabama, and even extending into Georgia and Mississippi on occasion.

With the carpetbaggers in control, and Mun with a background in the Federal army, he continued his lawless ways with virtual impunity, not being bothered much by law enforcement during that period as he went his merry way!

Although he was brushed by the law on several occasions, the wider range helped to dilute his impact on the countryside, with slow communications making it difficult for people to associate one of his crimes with another.

Free range, (*the practice of allowing livestock to range freely outside, while fencing the cultivated fields to keep the livestock out*) worked well in the practices of the Evans gang as stealing stock was relatively simple, either to drive it away on foot, or butcher it out and haul the meat away. This was one of his fields of endeavor.

The gang was mostly residue from the scout company, with some relatives, such as Benjamin F. and John H. Evans along with some newly freed slaves being participants. There isn't much evidence to indicate armed robbery, or violent crime of that type. They were more into booze making, smuggling, and selling, along with stock theft with an occasional murder caused by fear, meanness, or grudge, real or imagined. This was their method of operation.

After the war Mun tried to continue with business as usual, and with a surprising amount of success! Moonshine whiskey was a staple of his life from that time forward, including making, selling, and drinking. It might very well have influenced many of his later decisions, affecting incidents forming the fabric of his life. Some of the things done by the gang indicate decisions by either a drunk or a maniac, or perhaps even both, a drunken maniac!

With the departure from the scene of John Dickey, who had given William Monroe Evans a pretty low start, Mun started a long slide downward, even from that low start he already had. Who knows what level of depravity he would have reached had he lived to die of old age?

This, however, was not to be. There was that date with destiny that had to be kept by him, as well as his son John Henry Evans! The "hangmen were waiting in the wings", so to speak.

Suspended Sentence Chapter Two
Turmoil

With the end of the war came chaos as the carpetbagger regime came to power over the newly-defeated Confederacy. Law enforcement was at a shaky level, as the courts and all levels of local government were totally and completely reorganized, or disorganized was perhaps a more appropriate term, with political patronage at a level never heard of before nor since. There was a period of severe economic depression, the currency of the land was dead! Confederate Dollars, which had been seriously inflated during the war were now not even exchangeable for legal tender at *any* discounted rate. With the newly freed slaves competing with the returning Civil War veterans of both the Blue and Gray in the very weak job market, starvation was a realistic specter to many people of the South.

This situation was in effect at the time of the disappearance of John Dickey. After the depredations wrought upon the local populace during the war, he wisely disappeared, at any rate from his old familiar haunts. He apparently maintained a low profile for the rest of his days, living off his ill-gotten gains and working as a tanner. He had accumulated an impressive estate of $6000 value, and that was from combined Federal wages as a scout and loot from his illicit enterprises throughout the war, most likely.

Information emerges by bits and dribbles on the affairs of Mun Evans, but it wasn't long after the war that he organized a so-called "self-protection" group, comprised of some of the same outlaws with whom he had spent the war, along with several newly freed black slaves, and their lawlessness ran rampant.

Through some kind of feud or disagreement with the local population Evans decided, probably as a prelude to extortion of funds in some manner, to emphatically get the attention of everyone. One of his notable undertakings in 1869 was to prepare for his gang to blow up the Methodist Church in Paint Rock, during religious services. It is located North of New Hope, Alabama, where the Masonic Hall also was to be leveled by explosives William Monroe Evans would furnish at or near the same time.

Unfortunately for the Evans gang, but fortunately for the local citizenry, one of the Negroes let the cat out of the bag, which resulted in a warrant being issued, and a "strong posse" being formed for the purpose of executing the warrant. A.M. Nabors, one informant, tells us that he was a member of this "strong posse" under a deputy sheriff. It seems that the leader of said posse was Willis C. Stephens, a former member of the John Dickey outfit as well as a brother to Mary Polly (Stephens), who was as far as I can determine the common law wife of William Monroe Evans, as I was unable to find records of their marriage. Again, word leaked out, and the gang left at top speed, just eluding the posse, which followed in hot pursuit.

The game of tag lasted for a little over a week in the mountains around Guntersville, according to Nabors, with which Evans was no doubt more familiar than the posse, as he had grown up in that area.

The pursuit finally ended at a place called Wild Goat Cove, near Fearn's Ferry, which is in turn near Guntersville, Alabama, on the Tennessee River. At last the posse met with some success, they overtook some or all of the gang, and immediately fighting broke out, with six of the Negroes being either killed outright, or succumbing to their wounds shortly afterwards, per Nabors. It seems Nabors was the only person to see these six dead Negroes, which makes one wonder if he were really there, or had a vivid imagination!

There is another version of this story, which we will deal with, as well. This is from the other, better documented version of the confrontation at Wild Goat Cove. During the fracas, William Monroe Evans was wounded in the arm, but managed to escape into the surrounding rough terrain, and elude the efforts of the posse to find and capture him. He was even reported by his brother John Henry Evans, who was also in attendance, to have been killed at Wild Goat Cove. The report of his death by his brother could have been sincere, or used as a diversion to take attention away from Mun, giving him a chance to recover without the pursuit that might have occurred had he been thought to be alive.

With the type of resilience that type seems to

show so often, he did indeed survive to recover, but things were a trifle tight for him there now in Marshall County, and this engendered a move to the Southern end of Morgan County a little later, where he maintained a residence for the rest of his life.

Much of this information is due to the aforementioned A.M. Nabors. According to his story, this must have happened sixteen years before August 15, 1891, which would date it somewhere around 1875, although Mun still showed up in the 1880 Marshall County census with family. This seems to indicate an error or conflict in the time of this occurrence.

The Civil War ended in 1865, so he had apparently enjoyed freedom from threat for those intervening years (*Actually, the episode at Wild Goat Cove occurred on April 23, in 1869*). It might also reflect upon the reliability of Nabors' information in other matters.

In a letter to Headquarters Camp at McClung's Springs comes a report from Capt. (Brevet Major) George H. McLoughlin, dated 24 April, 1869. He reports the arrival of John Henry Evans in his camp, with Evans' word that he "had to fly from Wild Goat Cove yesterday". He further reported that Willis Stevens, a white man, had a company of about 34 colored men, and had skirmished with some white men who called themselves Ku Klux Klan. One of the white men, William Monroe Evans, was killed, one colored man, Henry Rivers was wounded, and the fight was still raging.

William Monroe Evans was reported by Nabors

to have married the daughter of Nicholas Stephens, of Marshall County. Research indicates her name was Mary, or Polly, as she was also known. *(The above mentioned Willis C. Stevens is her brother, a son of Nicholas Stephens, or Stevens. Both spellings were used from time to time but Stephens is the correct version the family used)* The story seems true in a limited way, they did indeed spend the rest of **his** life together, living in Southern Morgan County, about a mile from Welcome Falls *(known at that time simply as "The Falls")* until his untimely death in 1891, although I haven't been able to find any indication that he ever married her, or anyone else, for that matter!

An affidavit by W.C. Stephens dated August 26, 1869, is in regard to a try at arresting W.M. Evans, John Evans, Robert Ice, Burgers Finnell, and Green Horton on the 21st of August, 1869, for disguising themselves and going to a home and forcibly taking a shotgun. *(This was the home of Nicholas Stephens)*

George H. McLoughlin reports "On the 21st of August, 1869, I had a warrant, and tried to arrest on it W.M. Evans, John Evans, (white), Robert Ice, (colored), Burgers Finnell and Greene Horton, (colored). I arrested Finnell and Horton. I also arrested W.M. Evans, but he succeeded in getting away".

The warrant for arrest was issued against the above-named men for disguising themselves and going to the home of N. Stevens (*"my father", statement of W.C. Stephens*) and forcibly taking from him a shot-gun.

"On Monday last, the 23rd of August, I summoned about twenty men as a *posse comitatus,* (they were white and black) and attempted to arrest W.M. Evans (white) and Bob Ice (colored.) They were at Squire Bronson's, at Wild Goat Cove. I surrounded the house, but they broke and run out the back part of it, accompanied by Ben Evans, his brother. They were halted by a colored man (one of my posse) named Elliot Cottrell, when L.A. Bronson leveled his gun and fired at Cottrell, wounding him slightly. Cottrell and the others then fired, shooting W.M. Evans in the arm. The parties then got away, and up to this date I have not succeeded in arresting them. All of this was at Wild Goat Cove, near Fearn's Ferry, Alabama".

(*signed*) W.C. Stephens.
(witnessed by O.H. Morrow)

This affidavit was sworn and subscribed to before me, an officer of the United States Army, at McClung's Spring, Alabama, August 26, 1869.

Captain George H. McLoughlin.

Captain Second Infantry, Brevet Major, U.S.A.

A true copy: James Miller

First Lieutenant Second Infantry, Post Adjutant

Affidavit pertaining to Moses Sullivan, Marshall County

"On the 23rd day of August, 1869, I was returning from my brother's, to where I live, about two miles and one half from Deposit, (Fort Deposit) toward Vienna. Two men met me on the road; one of them was white, the other a mulatto. I believe that the white man's name was Benjamin Evans, the colored man's name was Bob Ice. The white man cocked his rifle and fired at me, the ball passing through my thigh. I never gave the man any provocation to shoot me." (Signed with an "X" as "His Mark") Henry Rivers.

According to a story I picked up, probably not documentable, the disguising of the group and the taking of the shotgun of Nicholas Stephens was because of William Monroe Evans' seduction of a sister of W.C. Stephens, daughter of Nicholas Stephens, from whom the shotgun was taken. She was also, then, a sister to Mary Polly Stephens, the probably common law wife of William Monroe Evans, or even more likely it was Mary Polly Stephens herself!

One folklore account had William Monroe Evans taking Mary Polly from her father's home at gun point, but confirmation on this is shaky. Another has him shooting the father for possession of the daughter. This version is patently untrue! These stories are probably several years younger than the happening, being created by some to make the story more interesting. I haven't found any credible corroborating information to that effect.

Following the above conflict a letter was written from Vienna, Alabama on September 18, 1869. It reads:

Dear Sir:

We, the undersigned, citizens of Vienna and vicinity, in view of the existing state of affairs in Marshall County, adjacent to this section, to wit, the murders and other outrages that have recently been committed in said county, and threats of violence upon this place and vicinity, thereby rendering life and property insecure, and having a desire for peace, order, and quiet, do respectfully petition you to send a sufficient force of United States soldiers to this place immediately.

Very respectfully,

Robert W. Peevy	A. Whited
J.W. Grayson	D.W. Parker
Lot S. Ledbetter	James Latham
J.M. Ledbetter	James Edge
James L. Ledbetter	H.B. Gabor
J.G. Ellett	W.D. Collins
Isaac D. Wann	*S.M. Nabors*
R.E. Cochron	S.W. Kennemore
J.H. Alchley	B.A. Nowlin
Joseph W. Grayson	F.M. Stone
F.T. Butler	E.C. Lusk
James W. Allison	Jacob Owens
Henry Wann	G.L.T. Lusk
John T. Haden	Louis Vann

T.M. Finnell   *J.B. Dickey*
Joseph A. Haden   W.P. Lusk
B.F. Walker

This petition was sent to Major General Crawford, commanding United States Forces at Huntsville, Alabama.

The italicized names: *J.G. Ellett*, a rather rare name, is probably related to Volney Ellett, who reportedly died at the hands of the Dickey contingent. *(Jack Dickey tells me there are still Elletts in the New Hope area). S.M. Nabors* is likely our A. M. Nabors, writer of the letter to the Alabama Tribune. If not, he is almost surely a relative of his. *J.B. Dickey*, while of the surname, is not our John W. Dickey, the renegade spy, but very likely a relative of that John. Other surnames seem to match others in the list of outlaws, as well!

A move was made, but not a very clean move, to Morgan County, Alabama by William Monroe Evans. He maintained at least two extra-curricular families during that time, probably more, with one being at Brown's Valley, Marshall County, very near where he grew up, and the other in the vicinity of Lacy's Spring, located on US 231 , just South of the Tennessee River, across from Huntsville, Alabama. He is reputed to have fathered some sixty to seventy children during his life, by several women.

Lacy's Spring is in the edge of Morgan County. Was he playing County lines, so he could flee easily the jurisdiction of those who might come to arrest him by going into the adjacent county, as he did in Morgan County during the remainder of his life?

An interesting note about Lacy's Spring: It was named for Hopkins Lacy, a member of it's earliest family, surname spelled in this manner, but the early post office ordered a rubber stamp which came back with an error of the spelling, and since that time it has been Lacey's Spring!

William Monroe Evans claimed to be a Mormon, but it was difficult to find any kind of religion in his actions. It seems to have been the best excuse he could come up with on short notice for his practice of promiscuous polygamy. He was reported by Nabors to misquote the Bible, convincing his wife he was entitled to as many women as he wanted.

A strange aspect of his Bible-reading talents is shown in some mortgages I have in my possession, by which he borrowed money from one Mikel Crawford, for one, who at one time or another held a mortgage on virtually every farm in that part of the county, I'm sure. These mortgages were signed with an "X" by both William Monroe and Mary Polly Evans, with the names written in the handwriting of Miles Humphries with the notation "His mark" and "Her mark". It must have been a very interesting presentation, his reading from the Scriptures when he couldn't even read and write his own name!

As to their marriage, I have been unable to find any indication that there was a marriage in either of the four most logical counties, Blount, Marshall, Madison, and Morgan. It is possible that they went somewhere else and got married, but I find that rather unlikely, based upon his life style! I found no record of marriage by the son, John Henry Evans, either, although he reportedly maintained illicit families paralleling those of his father.

Throughout this stretch of years, Mun Evans acquired a reputation as a thief of livestock, with special emphasis on hogs. The rule of that day was, as previously mentioned, free range, and Mun found this ideal for his type of operation, with animals very easy to steal, transport, and dispose of, with it being quite easy to make a profit by selling something he had paid nothing for!

Since the country was rather heavily wooded at that time, theft of livestock was rather simple if you had the ruthless audacity of Mun Evans! He didn't hesitate to butcher someone's milk cow, taking the choice cuts of meat to feed himself and his traveling companions, simply leaving the rest of the carcass, along with the hide and bell she was wearing, where it could easily be found and identified after the rest of the meat had spoiled! Petty and mean thievery of this type was his specialty!

Another device he used was for his gang to fire their guns into the houses of people, and under cover of this diversion, drive away the prized stock belonging to the people and kept inside their barns for safety from such as Mun's gang.

One reason he was able to survive for so long was that he and his gang covered a rather large area of country, raiding in all of Northern Alabama, even venturing into Mississippi, Tennessee, and Georgia on occasion.

As the years rolled on, confidence seemed to grow by leaps and bounds in William Monroe Evans. He had gone virtually unchallenged for a long time, and wore his arrogance like a halo, quick to pounce on anyone defenseless who even thought about disagreeing with him.

An incident occurred near Simcoe, Alabama, located between the Evans residence and Cullman, that hardened the attitudes of the general populace toward Evans and his gang. William Monroe Evans, in the company of three others (unnamed) were riding along the road returning from Cullman when they spotted some school children walking home from school. There seems to have been a feud, or disagreement between a Mr. Kemp, or Camp, and Evans, who thought Camp's son was in the group of children, and to get back at Camp, the four of them rode their horses at full speed through the group of children, as they fled for their lives.

The children injured most severely were George Schniteker, son of Herman and Dora (Linderman) Schniteker. Herman came from Germany to Texas at the age of 16 years.

George had his scalp severely torn, the laceration removing much of one ear as the horse tried vainly to jump over the boy, and hit him with it's hoof. He was reported to be a little "off" for the rest of his life as a result of the horse's hoof striking his head, but married and raised a family , so the effects were apparently not insurmountable for him.

Gus Linderman was also injured. The extent of his injuries are not known. The mother (*born Linderman*) of Mr. Edward Zinsmeister, still living in the Simcoe area today, was injured to the point that she carried a crippled arm to her grave, after having lived to be elderly. Children of both family names, Linderman and Schniteker, are buried in the Brindley Cemetery, located at the old Brindley Homestead, the place where Mace Thomas Payne Brindley, namesake for Brindley Mountain, raised his family. It is North of Simcoe, on the old Section Line Road.

It seems almost grimly ironic that damage, if any, to Camp's child or children was not reported. They probably were not even in the group!

The Linderman children's father was a former Indian fighter in the southwestern United States, and was instrumental in planning the demise of the pair of Evanses, although he apparently was not among those accused of lynching them.

He helped to set up a "watch and warning" system to help keep track of the comings and goings of the Evanses, which was accepted gladly by the people, as the threat of the pair was becoming ever more ominous!

According to Charles J. Humphries, a Mr. Zinsmeister, of the Cullman area, was a very prolific writer of letters to the editor over the years and wrote often on this subject. (from 1993 interview with Charles Humphries)

This was the kind of brazen act Mun was noted for, and as time went by people started to look for ways to protect themselves, along with their families and property from such incursions.

One example of his straying from the straight and narrow path is the warrant that follows:

Monroe Evans Indictment

The State of Alabama vs. Monroe Evans
No. 267 C.P.C. *(I simply don't know what C.P.C. means)*

For indictment in this case see Indictment Record Page 28.
The State of Alabama, Cullman County
(*The above indictment record is not available*)

To any sheriff of the State of Alabama Greeting: An indictment having been found against Monroe Evans at the spring term 1886 of the Circuit Court of Cullman County for the offense of carrying a pistol concealed about his person.

You are therefore commanded forthwith to arrest said defendant and to commit him to jail, unless he give bail to answer such indictment at the present term of our Circuit Court now in session in said County and make return of the writ according to law. Witness my hand this 30th day of April, 1886.

Julius Damus, Clerk of Circuit Court

Executed by arresting the within named defendant and bringing him in Court.

(signed) A.J. York, Sheriff

There was a sharp contrast in behavior when he was around home in Morgan County. My grandfather, Benjamin Franklin Holmes, knew him, and didn't find him that undesirable as a neighbor two miles away, (pretty near at that time), according to his son, Willard Coleman Holmes, but that didn't seem to hold true when he was out raiding! Also, their style seemed to change later, when son John grew into being a threat to the community in which he lived!

Mun had children by women in at least the three locations previously mentioned, and some children and other family members without names are buried in the Evans Cemetery, located between the Evans home and the Welcome falls. One is the daughter named either Molly or Milona. This is also the final resting place of William Monroe and John Henry Evans.

There is not a stone with so much as one letter on it in that cemetery, where I believe there are eight graves, with seven of them oriented in the traditional manner, with head to the West, while one, apparently an infant from the spacing of the head and foot stones, is oriented North and South, without a clear indication of which end is the head. I asked my mother, and she told me the reason the one little grave was oriented North and South was that the infant died in the summer, when the field was planted in corn, and rather than dig up a stalk or two of corn, they buried it between two rows of corn!

When I was a young man I felt a fascination for that old cemetery, and used to pass it fairly often while out rabbit hunting, and I used to stop and meditate there about what manner of people, what kind of circumstances, led to it's creation. It stood under a scrub cedar tree out in a cultivated field at that time, but is in a pasture belonging to Thomas D. Holcomb now, the third generation of the Holcomb family to own the property.

There doesn't seem to be any way to accurately ascertain just who is buried there, as the graves are unmarked, and it has been too long to expect to find first hand knowledge. It has always been known to me and everyone else in that community as the Evans Graveyard, but I don't even know for sure which graves are occupied by William Monroe and John Henry Evans! The cemetery is now located in a pasture (1997) overlooking, except for the trees blocking the view, the creek leading to Welcome Falls, and a truly beautiful view of the opposite side of the hollow, and even the Welcome Falls them-selves, although it is doubtful the actual falls were ever visible from that location due to the timber.

This is truly a beautiful place, the Welcome Falls stream, and the abyss into which it disappears be-tween the bluffs on it's way to it's rendezvous with the Tennessee River, past a place to the right of the stream about a mile down from the falls, known as Horse Thief Cave, where reportedly at one time a horse thief used the cave as living quarters while he allowed stolen horses to "cool off", and waited for altered brands to heal so they could be safely removed from the country.

If indeed this really did happen, it would have had to be in the early nineteenth century or sooner. It may just be something that was invented for entertainment. It is a beautiful place, either way, and was fun for a boy such as I to explore!

The remoteness of Horse Thief Cave would have lent itself to Mun's reputed moonshine operation, and I'm sure a lot of it was done back there in that area. I have gone there many times during my youth. The cave, while not colorful in scenery, was an attraction to a boy such as I! It was at one time a place for the youth of the community to go for a Sunday outing, using the cave to play our own version of the game known as "chicken", daring each other to go farther back into the cave.

There is a rock, a rather large boulder, lying on the floor inside the cave just a short distance from the entrance, and my mother told me that it was a part of the ceiling when she was a young girl. It might have been dislodged by a minor earthquake, or maybe just got tired and fell. That gives one food for thought when entering such a place!

This area is the setting where William Monroe Evans claimed headquarters and residence for the remainder of his natural life.

Suspended Sentence Chapter Three

The Life and Times of "Mun" Evans

For several years the Evans gang was accused of various crimes, with little or no successful prosecution, as they would leave the scene of a crime and go to one of the extra-curricular families, who had been coached and trained in the art of perjury, giving them a very solid-looking alibi by swearing they couldn't have been at the scene of the crime, as they had been with them all of the time. This made conviction very difficult, even impossible in most cases. Specifics pertaining to their crimes are sketchy, at best. The available folklore information is very hard to nail down to a specific source, as it wasn't too healthy to speak against William Monroe Evans!

One story that came down to me via folklore, for want of a better name, had to do with a peddler who came into the community to sell his wares. There are two versions of the story, I will try to remain in touch with both.

One story is that the man was a foot peddler, carrying his goods on his back as he walked through the country from door to door, spending the night with someone wherever night overtook him. He came into the country, but there was no indication or word that he ever left, indicating the probability of foul play.

At that time the road went across Welcome Falls,

just above the precipice, and underneath the edge, where the water spilled over, and something like ten feet down, is a ledge, starting from the North side of the falls, extending out under the falls, but feathering out, not going all the way across.

I am not sure when the discovery was made, but a human skeleton was found out on that ledge. It couldn't have been too easy, nor too secure either, going out on that ledge carrying a body. I was always afraid as a boy to go out there unencumbered, as there is still a drop of about thirty or forty feet from the ledge to the rocky pool below, although some of the other more daring souls among my peers did go out there.

The other possibility is that he might have gone out there under his own power, in an obviously vain attempt to escape attack, whether by the Evanses or others, as portrayed by Joan Mims..

My mother told me this version of the story, but she didn't know when that discovery was made, whether before or after the Evanses died. Obviously, if they did murder him, then it was before they died, but it might or might not have been discovered right away, and might not have been discovered for several years. Skeletal remains indicate it had been a while.

The best information I have on the peddler himself is a kind of folklore rumor, which states that he was from Tennessee, but he doesn't have a name in that report, and the skeleton was never identified, at least in part due to the primitive state of forensic science at that time. Unless there was a really outstanding characteristic, such as a row of gold teeth in front, which the Evanses would have probably taken anyway, it would have been just about impossible to identify the skeleton.

The other version of the story states that William Monroe Evans was seen driving the old peddler's horse and buggy shortly after he had disappeared. This would, if true, rule out the back-packing foot peddler. I personally believe the foot peddler version, as I have heard it all of my life from my mother and her family. If indeed it is true, that takes care of the "horse and buggy" tale!

So far, I haven't come up with the slightest lead as to the disposition that was made of the skeleton, whether the authorities were called in from Decatur, the county seat of Morgan County, or if the local people just quietly buried it somewhere locally.

All of us as youngsters knew the story, and the Falls Hollow was pretty desolate at the time of my youth, with no houses for half a mile or more. It used to be a boy's claim to manhood to walk through that hollow at night alone, and believe me, I still remember well the first time I did it!

The road ran across the brink of the falls at the time the Evanses lived there, and went North from there, up a draw, and back into the road that is there today where the old Cobbs Schoolhouse stood. That has been a lot of years.

The school children formally walked in a procession, or group from the old Cobbs Schoolhouse to

Gum Pond when the school was moved to the newly completed Gum Pond School, per Mr. Will Smith, who attended school there somewhere just before 1910, or thereabouts, along with my mother and some of her siblings. I have a picture of the teacher and student body taken at that time in front of Gum Pond School. My mother was there, too, in that gathering!

The road then continued in a Northerly direction, past the Frank Holmes place, where my grandfather, Benjamin Franklin Holmes raised his family, which was also the site of the Cotaco post office where he was postmaster from about 1900 to 1907, when the Cotaco post office was closed, and mail service for the community was transferred to Eva, Alabama.

From there it went on past the home of John Ealy Ryan, on down the mountain past the "rock patch" (named for the profusion that must have made cultivation a nightmare, but it was cultivated, nonetheless at one time), past the Jonathan Cobbs house at the mouth of "Dry Creek", where it enters Cotaco Creek, and passing near the old Cisero Taylor home, with it's attending forlorn cemetery long in disuse. It crossed the creek near the old "Ed'ard (Edward) Smith" place, and joined up with a road roughly paralleling what is SR 67 today. The Evanses traveled this road into the Florette, Alabama area, going cross country from there to meet present day SR 36, following it to one of their extracurricular families at Lacey's Spring.

It is mentioned in some source material that

William Monroe Evans was engaged in trafficking moonshine whisky, He was reported to descend upon anyone who even *thought* of turning him in, like the wrath of God, with at least one person being whipped "almost to death" by the Evanses.

Apparently they were engaged in some kind of legitimate farming, due to the mortgages in my possession that were recorded in Morgan County under his "x". In one document he borrows $893.75 from Mikel Crawford. This is signed, or "marked" by both W.M. and Polly Evans, and both used an "x".

It was due to be paid back by November 20, 1889, secured by described real estate. There seems to be a discrepancy in the amount of money, with the numbers reading "In the sum of 893.75", while written out it is "Ninety-three and 75/100 Cents Dollars. I am inclined to believe the lesser amount, as I can't visualize him being able to float nearly a thousand dollar loan.

Then in Somerville, Alabama on February 1st, 1877, we find a mortgage to W.B. Goodson in the amount of $125.00 to be paid at Somerville April the 30th, 1877. This is noted "for the purpose of securing more fully" property consisting of 160 acres of land described to wit, also "one dark chestnut sorrel horse 9 years old, one white cow, red neck, one dark brindle cow, ten head of hogs to have and to hold to the said W.B. Goodson, his heirs and assigns forever. Upon condition, however, that if I appear at the next turn of the Circuit Court and from day to day during said time until discharged on or before the said day of 1877, when the same falls due then this conveyance is to be void, but if I fail to appear at said time, then the said W.B.Goodson or agent or proper owner of said note, should it be transferred, is hereby authorized to take possession of said property above described, and after giving 10 days notice of time and place of sale by posting three written or printed notices, in as many public place in said county, to sell the same to the highest bidder for cash at Winfrey's Mill and to execute titles to purchasers, and to devote the proceeds of said sale to the payment 1st of the expense of acquiring possession, care of same until the time of sale, advertising, selling, and conveying, 2nd, of the amount with interest that may be due on said note, and lastly, if there be any surplus of said proceeds, the same is to be returned to the undersigned. Witness my hand and seal this the 1st day of February, 1877. (Followed by the names W.M. Evans and Mary Evans, each accompanied by an "x" described as "His Mark" and "Her Mark".

Witness:

C.W. Rice
Wm. Simpson
G.T. Whittle, J.P. Goodson

Signed before me satisfied this Feb. 2th (sic) 1877

E.M. Humphries,
Justice of the Peace.

This is clearly a loan being floated for bail

money, if you will notice the court appearances described above. That was more or less a way of life with William Monroe Evans, and no doubt happened many times with variations. This document doesn't give us any insight into the charges being brought against him, but you can bet it was something! The indictment isn't readily available in the record.

The old log cabin belonging to the above mentioned Miles Humphries still stands between Baileyton and Welcome Church. There was once a rather fancy (*for that day*) two story house standing in front and to the right of it, as you face it from the road.

This is the same Miles Humphries whose sister, Ann Humphries, married James Huston "Huse" Holmes. Huse was my great uncle.

In 1993 I had the pleasure of entering the old Miles Humphries cabin , and taking pictures there, but unfortunately the interior had been gutted, with the mantle from over the fireplace being outside, on the back porch. The cabin was apparently built by Miles Humphries and a man known as "Uncle Free" Bryant.

The Welcome Church near the old cabin is the source of the name "Welcome Falls". At the time of the happenings chronicled here, there was a road that ran from the old Humphries cabin cross-country to the Evans home, but that road has long been gone, to the extent that I saw no visible signs of it's ever having existed.

I have been unable to locate a picture of the old Evans house, although I saw it many times when I

This is E.M. Humphries, brother-in-law to James Huston Holmes, as well as being the coffin maker for the Evans duo. He was taught to read and write by his second wife, and worked for the rest of his life as a scribe, writhing out mortgages and other such papers in long hand.

was a lad, I didn't know at that time that was where they lived. I was able to see that old house across a hollow from fields I plowed in then, although it was about a mile away.

Although the road where the house stood is rather

heavily populated now, I am not sure who their next door neighbors would have been then. I thought for a while it would have been Jesse Van Holcomb and his wife Mary Elizabeth (Slaten) Holcomb, but they didn't move to the house I was thinking of until after the lynching. They still might have been the next door neighbors, but that was when they lived across the Falls Hollow, in the home (place) currently owned by Willard Holmes. The old house has been replaced for many years. (My own family lived in the old one for a while back during the depression)

In the other direction, their nearest neighbor is harder to name with accuracy. It *could* have been W.F.Knopp, about a mile away, but I'm not sure.

The people were pretty scattered at that time around that part of the country, with those I can name being Joseph Heinchie Creel and his wife Elizabeth "Lizzy" (Andrews) Creel, and there was W.T. Cobbs and his wife Cintha (Oden) Cobbs (a sister to my great grandmother). Then Ephraim Anders Jones moved into the community from Tallapoosa County, with his wife, Sephronia (Ransom) Jones and children. (He was my great-grandfather)

Benjamin Franklin Holmes, my grandfather, married as his second wife Frances Josephine (Jones) (Durham) Holmes, daughter of Ephraim Anders Jones. He then bought what became known as the old Holmes place where he raised his family from Marshall Cobbs, brother of Jonathon Cobbs. Marshall's wife and Benjamin Franklin's first wife were sisters named Wright, with Marshall marrying

Martha "Mattie" Wright, and Benjamin Franklin marrying Sarah Jane Wright. Marshall Cobbs moved to California after selling the farm to Benjamin Franklin Holmes. This place is now located on Hopper Road.

I haven't heard much about the neighbors visiting with the Evanses and vice versa, it probably occurred in a limited way.

I am still not very well satisfied with my knowledge of the Evans family, and where they went to disappear so suddenly after the unfortunate climax to this event. My mother had no idea where they might have moved to, nor did she know who is resting in the family cemetery, other than William Monroe and John Henry Evans, his son. In the future I am still hopeful of finding more information, hopefully I will be able to clear up at least some of these questions.

The Peddler

(How it Might Have Been)
by Joan Mims

The star represents the approximate location of the old peddler's skeletal remains. The scene here is what is today known as the "Welcome Falls", named for a church in the area, which did not exist at the time of the Evans lynching, this place being known simply as "The Falls". At that time the road ran across the top of the falls, with traffic on the road being almost visible from where this photo was taken.

The stillness and quiet of the woods was more straining on the ears than a loud noise! No birdsong was heard, and only once was there a sign of another living creature, a small rabbit had jumped out in the path of the buggy. Caroline screamed, a short, nervous, high-pitched sound. The horse raised it's forefeet and pitched, first to one side, then the other, almost upsetting the buggy. John brought it under control, and with curses under his breath he applied the whip several times, forcing the horse down the narrow road to the falls.

The clop-clop of the horse's feet kept time with the girl's heartbeat. There was a definite urgency to their pace. The spring rains had the small creek swollen to the top of it's banks and overflowing when there was a low area to escape into, and the old "Baptizin' Hole" was flooded, with the overflow making the creek flowing over the falls bigger than it had ever seemed before.

Driving the buggy as close to the edge of the falls as he dared, John pulled back on the brake, tossed the reins to Caroline, and leaped out, miring to his ankles in the soft ground beside the solid rock creek bed.

He pulled a jug of whiskey from under a quilt in the back of the buggy. Hooking a thumb through the handle, he slung it over his shoulder and drank his fill. Ramming the corn cob stopper back in the neck of the jug, he attended to the business at hand.

He reached under the quilt and dragged out another object that made a loud thud as it hit the ground. He gave a vicious kick to it's middle, which was the body of a man! John knelt down beside it and started rummaging through the pockets. A modest roll of money was found, an old Henry Sears knife, a pocket watch, and several coins, all of which made it's way into his own pockets.

John then climbed back into the buggy, where a white-faced Caroline was sitting, just as she was when the buggy stopped. Her fingers were white at the knuckles as she still clutched the buggy seat, a look of horror stamped on her face.

Many things were racing through her mind just now, one of which was what she was doing here with this man whom she thought she loved, thought she knew, and now knew as a murderer! How could she live like this when she had been brought up so differently? She had to get away!

Her grandfather was still living at the old home place on the Douglas road with no one to cook and wash for him. He was old and lonely, and would gladly take her in.

The life she had with John was bold and outrageous in this year of 1890, but it had it's moments. Imagine living under the same roof with a man's wife! While spending time with her, his wife and the children went on with the normal everyday chores. It had always caused a weird kind of excitement in her, but today a murder had been committed, and murder was another matter!

There had to be a plan. She'd have to be very careful or she could be the next victim. A human life meant nothing to John Henry Evans...No more than butchering a hog!

Her thoughts were suddenly cut short as John jerked the buggy sharply, miring into the mud and leaving deep trenches that were quickly filling with water. He whipped the horse into a frenzy, the buggy lurched forward and they went racing away along the sodden road.

The brown, huddled heap awoke with a jolt, the heavy scent of earth in his nostrils and the taste of blood in his mouth. The pain was unbearable, coming from all directions. The blood oozing from his vest had made a great puddle when he lifted himself up. Faint from loss of blood, he fell back to the ground and lay still, with only his labored breathing, the rise and fall of lungs at work, being the sole evidence that he was still alive.

The faraway whinny of a horse stilled his breathing for a few seconds and prompted him to start crawling. He inched his way along the edge of the falls, where the water from the creek disappeared into the abyss below.

He came upon a series of ledges six to eight feet high on the North side of the creek, and clinging to the edge of the first one, he dropped to the level below, and discovered that it led out under the waterfall, running along the face of the cliff beneath the sheltering rock above.

His only goal was to get away, to hide from the fiend who had done this hideous thing to him. One inch at a time he crawled, seeming like an eternity. Finally coming to the end of the ledge, where it narrowed and faded into the sheer face of the cliff, and well out of sight of anyone looking from the top of the falls, he lay in the grip of exhaustion. The wild Hydrangea, or "seven bark" bushes would hide him from the view of anyone looking from the walls of the canyon. He must rest! If he could just stay hidden long enough to regain his strength, then he might make it back out to the road and find help. He was very light-headed, and sheets of blackness were overtaking him, then he slipped into oblivion.

He awoke to a cold, gray dawn. Streaks of light were beginning to show in the East, he realized he had been unconscious all night. The spray from the falls had soaked his clothes, and an uncontrollable shiver wracked his frame. Pain permeated his body, and it was more than he could stand. After a brief battle with it, he closed his eyes again, forever!

The squealing could be heard all the way to the Evans Cemetery, on what would become the Jesse Van Holcomb farm, as the trio of young boys splashed in the cold water of the "Baptizing" Hole". The first of May was a little too soon to be swimming, but some things just can't wait!

The winter had been long and rigorous, and it made it mighty hard to resist the lure of summer's highlight, the pool above the falls. The thought of fun in the woods, swimming and "swinging out" the hickory saplings and making hickory bark whistles was just too much to resist!

Birds were busy with the things that birds do in the springtime, bees hummed a hypnotic drone, and the promise of "creases" in the pot that night was foremost in each boy's head.

After the swim they made their way down the

rocks to the bottom of the falls, just as they had last year. Jesse laid his shirt down and filled it to the bursting point with water cress, growing in the pool at the bottom of the falls. Beautiful little birds were flitting around the cliff overhead, twigs clamped firmly in their beaks as they worked diligently on their nests.

The boys were all at the bottom of the canyon now, and were rubbing their legs, which were beginning to burn from climbing the saplings.

Two birds were scrambling in the vegetation on the highest ledge, just under the edge of the falls. Paul, who was a sensitive, dreamy sort of lad, was watching the birds, amazed at what they could do with their beaks. Just then, as the birds worked into the ground cover, he saw something white.

He asked the other boys if birds used large sticks to build their nests. No? Then what had he seen? They decided to climb back up to the top of the falls, then drop down to the ledge and see what it was. That small ledge area tapered off to nothing against the sheer rock face, but had vegetation growing on it. The boys inched their way along the ledge toward it's end, where they discovered a skeleton!

They ran to get Jesse's father, because he lived the closest, but he had gone to Baileyton that day. They decided, since it was Saturday, and grinding day, to go to the old grist mill on the old Evans place to tell someone what they had found. It was always a little spooky going past the old Evans Graveyard!

The Evanses, William Monroe and his son John

Henry, had been hanged by vigilantes in 1891, or so the story goes. There were six other family members buried there, as well. Some of the graves were quite small, so it was assumed that they were children. One child had died in the summertime, and had been buried in a grave oriented North and South, because the space that would have placed the body in the traditional direction, facing East, had corn planted in it. Seemingly the area was begrudged, and the family didn't want to disturb the corn that was growing there. It hadn't made sense to chop down the corn just to honor a tradition, so it was left and the child wedged in between the rows, lying in another direction!

Well, the whole neighborhood turned out at the falls, and the skeletal remains were stacked gently and carefully into an old cotton basket made of white oak "splits", and brought back off the ledge.

The story about the foot-peddler who turned up missing about eight years ago had re-surfaced, and was on the lips of everyone in the whole community. The autumn of 1890 was almost a year before what became known as the "Baileyton Lynching".

No one seemed to know who the old foot-peddler was, it was rumored that he came from Tennessee, but no one could narrow it down from there. The primitive state of forensic science made a positive identification impossible, his identity went with him to his grave!

The boys who found the skeleton were twelve years old in 1898, and would have been only four at the time of the disappearance of the peddler, and five at the time of the lynching. The people who were present at the hanging and other members of this small community passed down by word of mouth this story through intervening generations. No one is alive today who witnessed it, but the legend still lives on in the minds of their descendants as if it had happened yesterday!

Suspended Sentence Chapter Four
Chip off the old block!

In the year 1866 another blessed (?) event occurred, in the form of the birth of John Henry Evans.
There have been many discussions and arguments
about the merits and demerits of environment versus
heredity, but I guess the consensus of all those
arguers would be in agreement that a double infu-
sion of environment *AND* heredity would be much
more potent than either! Such was the lot of John
Henry Evans.

Information about his early years is sketchy, at
best, but like William Bonney, alias Billy the Kid,
his reputation would be made young or not at all. It
is difficult to establish the proper chronology of
events due to the scarcity of information, but he was
born in Brown's Valley, Marshall County, Alabama,
of William Monroe Evans and Mary Polly
(Stephens) Evans.

His father recruited him early into the lawless
paths that would be his element for the balance of
his short life. William Monroe Evans had other sons
by Mary Polly Stephens, as well as others without
names or number by other illicit wives (?). Apparently John Henry was the only son involved with his
father in a life of crime. I have no explanation for
that.

It is not clear just when he started his extra-
curricular families paralleling those of his father, but

it must have been pretty early, as he only attained the age of twenty-five years.

It is not the author's intention to impugn the family name of Evans, as there are many people of the name who are paragons of honor and decency, many figuring prominently into the development of this country. I know of no others of the name who could be compared to these two generations of this family in the annals of infamy! They just seemed to believe in doing everything wrong!

About the first time I find any track of John other than statistical information is the incident involving Pierce Mooney. The story, pretty well documented, is that he shot Pierce Mooney as he worked in his blacksmith shop, from ambush. His marksmanship is suspect, as he shot him in the leg. Martha Davis told me the Mooney family had the hat in their possession worn by Pierce Mooney at the shooting, with a bullet hole in it! She had seen the hat! This turned out to be only a slight error, as the hat she was referring to was worn by Pierce's father Martin H. "Boze" Mooney when he was shot a generation earlier.

After some research and a bit of luck, I also have seen the old home made beaver skin hat, via pictures. That is another story!

This shooting of Pierce Mooney may very well have been the beginning of the end for the father-son duo. The injured leg of Pierce, along with the treatment and threats that followed, fostered the chain of

Arrow points to the hole made by the bullet that took the life of Martin H. "Boze" Mooney when shot by a group of "Home Guards", a name used by those who avoided military service, staying home to loot and pillage.

This hat is held by the parents of Henry Mooney. Martin H. was abducted from his home in the present day Welcome Community and taken to the Ryan's Cross Roads area, where he was sat against a tree and shot to death.

events leading up to their deaths by hanging!

One must wonder why John would do such a thing, mere meanness wouldn't seem to explain it. Now we must fall back on the information gleaned in personal interviews, the only source of information in some cases.

There was a feud, or disagreement between the Evanses and the Mooneys impossible to trace to it's onset, but somewhere during it's course a gang of "Home Guards", a name for those looters and pillagers not in the army of either side, just staying clear of any danger while they lived off the fat of the land, took Pierce Mooney's father, Martin H. "Boze" Mooney (an elderly man, and also a blacksmith) prisoner at or near the Mooney home, and took him somewhere in the vicinity of Ryan's Crossroads, sat him down against a tree, and shot him to death. He was not found for about two weeks. The hat pictured is the one he was wearing when he was executed. This was not really out of character for this type of people. This could possibly have been some of the Dickey contingent, but is not really too likely.

He was called to account by a "fat man" for feeding those "lay-outs", or slackers from the Confederate Army, of which he didn't even have any knowledge!

Another interesting possibility for the beginning and cause of the Mooney-Evans feud might be the fact that Pierce Mooney married Mary M. Evans, whom I strongly suspect, but haven't been able to prove conclusively, was the older half-sister of

William Monroe Evans!

The most bizarre event was when they (the Evanses) went to Dr. G.W. McLarty's house and drew a picture of a coffin in the dirt of his front yard, with the message that he would die if he treated Pierce Mooney's wound inflicted by John Evans. He (John) wanted him to die of neglect, as his poor marksmanship had failed to do the job. They also reportedly threatened Mooney's wife for treating his wound, also!

While there is not a picture of Pierce Mooney available, I am including a picture of his son Franklin Mooney, taken about 1906.

Some of the undercurrents of these situations seem to indicate that the Evanses were engaged in the manufacture and distribution of illegal spirits (moonshine). There was a double threat to this business, one being that they would be reported to the authorities, the other being that other people might be competitive with them in quality, price, or availability. They were paranoid on both subjects.

The Goodlett brothers were other objects of the wrath of the Evanses. John and Ben Goodlett were apparently upstanding citizens who had somehow run afoul of the Evans wrath and were under the threat of death by John. I have no clue as to the reason for that.

Pierce Mooney swore out a warrant for John Evans over the ambush in Mooney's blacksmith shop, , and here is where the story goes in several directions. One version is that John took off after the

Goodlett brothers to murder them, and was intercepted by Justice of the Peace Matt Heaton, arrested, and placed under guard in the Baileyton Alliance Store, at Baileyton, Alabama, in Cullman County. After that happened, William Monroe Evans found out about it and went to the aid of his son. Upon reaching Baileyton, he was arrested even before dismounting from his horse. This placed them both under guard in the store.

Another version has William Monroe locked up in the Alliance Store after having been arrested in Brown's Valley, Marshall County for some unknown reason. Upon reaching Baileyton, it was late enough that they spent the night there, intending to go on to Cullman the following day. John, upon hearing of his father's detention, went to Baileyton to take supper to his father. It was searched, and found to contain not one, but two pistols, at which time he was also arrested and placed under guard with his father.

Both of these versions are somewhere in the vicinity of the truth, but I am able to put a lot more stock in the following version.

Pierce Mooney swore out a warrant for the arrest of John Henry Evans, and the warrant was placed in the hands of law enforcement officers. The habits and haunts of the Evans duo were well known, so the first place they looked was Brown's Valley, and there they found John Henry Evans. I will now give you two articles from the Guntersville Democrat, the first dated August 20th, 1891.

"The Democrat"

From Baileyton, Cullman County, about half way between Guntersville and Cullman, comes a story of a double lynching, said to have occurred on the night of the 15th, when Mun Evans and his boy John were hanged to a limb by a mob of citizens. The report says that last May a man named Mooney was shot at his shop by someone in ambush. For some time suspicion had rested on the two Evans. The arrest of the boy, John Evans, was made last week by Sheriff Wells in this county (Marshall), under orders from Cullman County officers who came after Evans. It seems the trial was before a Justice at Baileyton who is reported to have bound them over and while Bill Evans went to Cullman after bail for his relatives a mob took them out and hung them, father and son.

The Evans' are said to have been the parties who took a man out a few weeks since and whipped him almost to death. At this writing we have been able to obtain only meager particulars.

This article seems to have a lot to tell us about the situation! Now we know why John was being held prisoner in Baileyton! Also, let us make a note of the beating, or whipping, administered by the Evans pair. As we try to tie the points together that beating becomes very pivotal to the whole story.

Let us return now to the Guntersville Democrat for an article following the first one by a week, dated August 27, 1891.

"The Democrat"

Fuller particulars of the Cullman County necktie party confirm the report published in these columns last week. From persons living in the vicinity it is learned that Monroe Evans had been a man greatly dreaded by his neighbors. He was charged with running a wildcat still and making short work of anyone suspected of a tendency to inform the authorities It is further said that a few years ago he ran through a crowd of children while on horseback, wounding several of them with the horse's hoofs.

Several parties claim that Monroe Evans about the close of the *(Civil)* War armed a crowd of Negroes and incited them to take blasting powder, which he furnished, to blow up a Church at Paint Rock, in Madison County , which was crowded with people at worship. In the discovery of this plot and the subsequent attack on his party by the law abiding citizens it appears that Mason (sic) *(no doubt an error, meaning Monroe)* received several gunshot wounds.

If all of these facts are true, it is hardly probable that any amount of reward would tempt a citizen to turn informer.

"Those that live by the sword may expect to die by the sword" is a true saying! If Evans had been an upright and law-abiding citizen it is more than probable that he would be alive today.

This is typical of the documentation found wherever one chances to look. They were feared not because people were timid, but because of the threat they posed to individuals. They were most dangerous because they could pick the time and circumstances to attack, when the odds were all in their favor! The stories of their conduct, or more specifically their misconduct, are rife with cases of brutality.

One of their trademarks was the drawing of coffins in people's yards, as with Dr. G.W. McClarty. It was not unusual for them to wait for a woman to be alone and unprotected, , then break into the house, if necessary, to commit rape. One such case tells of an attempted break-in in which the lady of the house barred the door, then shot through a loophole provided for defense of the house, putting a bullet into the abdomen of William Monroe Evans. This is from an interview with Charles J. Humphries.

At any rate, we now understand some of the reasons why confinement of both Evanses at Baileyton attracted so much attention among the long-suffering public. I suppose I could have been enticed into the events that followed their incarceration at the Baileyton Alliance Store, had I had the safety of myself and my family at stake, as the lynch mob very likely felt they did!

The word spread quickly about the capture and confinement of the father and son. One can only speculate as to what happened in detail. About the first thing that happened was that an effort was made by sending people out for the ostensible purpose of borrowing guns for guarding the Evans duo against a breakout by their friends, or gang.

Riders went out to all points of the compass to that end, which was absurd on it's face, as there probably wasn't a home in the whole country without a gun, anyway, for hunting, killing vermin, snakes, etc.

The obvious reason was to spread the word about the coming event, which was **not** to hang them, but to administer a horse-whipping. Remember the Democrat article, about the man the Evanses had whipped almost to death? He was almost certainly, in my opinion, a member of the "White Caps", the same organization as the mob was formed of, and a subversive arm of the Ku Klux Klan forced underground by the Federal Government after it's creation following the Civil War to combat the thefts and depredations of the carpetbaggers.

It was a common practice for the carpetbaggers to elect fraudulently to office a figurehead Negro, then use him in whatever way necessary to manipulate the electorate to produce ill-gotten profits for the carpetbaggers. The Ku Klux Klan came into being to make those Negroes afraid to occupy such a post. This information or opinion, if such it might be called, was handed down to me by my grandfather, Samuel J. Bradford in conversation during my youth.

The lynching was not slated to be a killing! If you were going to hang someone, wouldn't you at least bring along a rope? I believe they were that smart, too! This was to be pay-back time for their member who had been so beaten by the Evanses!

There were at least two people who were notified who chose not to attend the event, probably feeling justifiably afraid that the thing would get out of hand, as it most certainly did! One of them was Joseph Heinchie Creel, who lived 7 Jan 1846/20 Jul 1913, buried at Etha Church Cemetery, alongside his wife, Sara Elizabeth "Lizzie" (Andrews) Creel, 11 Aug 1855/16 Aug 1931. He reportedly paced the floor all night without sleep that night after being notified.

The other was W.F. Knopp, the father of Elizabeth (Knopp) Creel (Mrs. George Creel). His final resting place is not known. He and his wife went on some kind of trip, probably to visit relatives, as that was the primary reason for such trips at that time, and unfortunately he died on the trip, and she had to bury him and return alone, which must have been heartbreaking.

No one knows for sure now where that was, but the best guess seems to be Randolph County, in the vicinity of Roanoke, Alabama. W.F. Knopp is mentioned in connection with Drum Creek Primitive Baptist Church in Marshall County, the Church had 18 members in 1876, dissolved in 1890. It is probably under water from the Tennessee River since the building of the Guntersville Dam. He was also a charter member of Old Canaan Church, In Cullman County.

Anyway, neither of them chose to attend the affair in Baileyton that night of August 15, 1891.

With the repercussions that followed, their worst fears were well grounded!

It is reported that parties of men were seen walking as well as riding horseback toward Baileyton on that afternoon and evening from all directions. One report came from Mabel (Holmes) Burks. The parents of her husband, Buford Burks, told her about hearing the hoofbeats of many horses going past their house in Baileyton that fateful night.

Apparently they met at some kind of staging area in or near Baileyton, because it seemed to go rather smoothly as their activity unfolded. A force able to smother the guards by sheer numbers came to and entered the Baileyton Alliance Store around ten o'clock on the Saturday night of August 15, 1891, a day that lodged Baileyton in the history books forever! The number of men has been estimated variously from twenty-five to two hundred men. It was no doubt between those two numbers!

The thing that made it look so easy, in my opinion, is that the whole thing was a set-up, with every last soul in the store, or near it, being in on the deal except the Evanses! Note that not a shot was fired, and no one was injured. Guns were removed from the hands of people supposedly alertly on guard!

The gang, friends of the Evanses, never materialized, only the White Caps, so called for the way they dressed. Do you think for a split second that the friends of the Evanses would have gained entry that easily?

The White Caps have been reported as far away

as Mississippi, probably the white headgear made it easier to tell friend from foe during night-time operations. There is also the possibility they might have been dressed any other way in Baileyton, though they were at least probably masked, as this wasn't a band of night-riding vigilantes, but the most substantial citizenry or the whole area, evidently doing a job that they had given up on expecting the duly authorized law enforcement agencies to do. It would be interesting to hear where the "White Caps" story originated. Was it an attempt to fix blame on someone other than themselves? The answers to such questions lie buried in cemeteries across the area.

The next several minutes after the arrival of the "White Caps" seemed to go better than any unrehearsed or uncooperative venture of that type could have gone! When it was over, everyone was firmly welded together in a conspiracy of silence, which held together through some very dedicated efforts by Governor Thomas Jones to fracture the shell of armor used by those who otherwise were very vulnerable.

Probably a gang of miscellaneous thugs could not have made such a conspiracy stick, but these were the elite of Baileyton society, as we shall see later.

It seems incredible that a group of armed men could have taken two prisoners from another group of armed men, who were supposedly alertly on guard, without a shot being fired, or even the most minor injury occurring to either side!

Where did this group of men come from, and

where did they go? The vast majority of them came from the immediate area of Baileyton, with some coming from as far away as ten miles or so. A lot of them went to Pleasant Grove, Lawrence's Chapel, Etha, and other cemeteries in the area eventually, but their short term destination was a relatively short distance down the road, to bed, and for many I'm sure, a sleepless night, one of many that was to follow.

Suspended Sentence Chapter Five
The boil festers!

On the day of August 15th, 1891, many things came together! Probably the most credible story pertaining to the way it all happened is the one where John Evans (Monroe Evans' boy, as stated in the Guntersville Democrat) was arrested in Marshall County by their Sheriff Wells, under papers brought to him by Cullman County officers, and taken to Baileyton, as a destination, not a stopover *en route* to Cullman. This happened Thursday, August thirteenth, 1891. He was placed under guard when he arrived in Baileyton at the Baileyton Alliance Store, which was owned by some kind of co-operative similar to the Farm Bureau and other Grange organizations owned by their members. The Alliance Store was managed by James Huston "Huse" Holmes, per his niece, Mabel (Holmes) Burks in interview.

Word got to William Monroe Evans that his son was being held prisoner there, and he immediately went to the Alliance Store to try to be of assistance to his son. Upon arrival, he was arrested even before he could dismount from his horse, by Justice of the Peace Matt Heaton.

They both, father and son, had unsavory reputations with the people of Baileyton, and were guarded apparently with enthusiasm. There didn't seem to be any shortage of people willing to guard them.

Everything seemed to be going smoothly, guards were in place both inside and outside the building,

The house above the star is on the location where Huse Holmes lived in 1891. Looking from the site of the old Alliance Store, you can see highway 69 in the foreground. The parents of Mabel (Holmes) Burks also lived on that road with Huse's house.

with replacement shifts readily available, some of them sleeping in the home of J.H. "Huse" Holmes, according to later testimony. It was turning into a quiet, uneventful night.

Will Evans had gone to Cullman to try to raise bond money "for his relatives". It is not perfectly clear who Will Evans was, but it is pretty sure that he was a son of William Monroe, and a brother to John Henry Evans. It is possible it could have been Mun's father, who was also named William Evans. Mun did have a son named William.

As the day faded into night, groups of armed men

71

were seen at several points, converging on Baileyton from all directions. While they were approaching, all seemed quiet and serene.

I have no account of it, but they must have met at a pre-determined rendezvous to assign roles, plan strategy, etc. before proceeding into the approaching drama. No one at or near the store where the prisoners were held seemed to suspect a thing, if you take things at face value. According to testimony following this night, some of them were asleep, awaiting their turn on guard in blissful ignorance of the events that were about to unfold. No one knows, nor will they ever know for sure just what happened in Baileyton that night, as to the involvement of people, the motivation, the planning committee, and other details taken to the grave with those who knew and participated. I will attempt to approach the situation with all of the information available, and some of the best logic available to me to fill the holes left by the actual information.

From a sleepy, dull, monotonous evening (*apparently*) the people in and around the Baileyton Alliance Store were rather rudely awakened! The Village of Baileyton was suddenly filled with armed men, the number variously estimated at from twenty-five to two hundred suddenly appearing at virtually all points in the area of the Baileyton Alliance Store. They were observed by E.S. Steward to be passing the home of Huse (James Huston) Holmes moving in the direction of the Alliance Store. His residence was across SR 69, by something like a hundred yards. The road was shaped like a "T", with his house being in line with that road, and across the road that makes up the cross for the "T". The site of his house is visible from the site of the old Alliance Store.

Steward ran out and was halted by the approaching men, then taken along to the store building where the prisoners were held, and kept in custody of the mob for about twenty minutes before being told to go on back to bed, and to stay there out of the way.

Suddenly, like a bolt from the blue the mob was upon the guards at the store! J.A. "Johnny" Hendrix was suddenly seized and thrown bodily across the road which is now SR 69. As he later related in private conversation, there was only one man in that whole country who could have performed that kind of feat of strength, and that man was William Ben Donaldson. Much later, after Donaldson had become an old man, he was still capable of holding up the front end of a tractor while the front tires were being changed!

G.C. Steward was sitting in the door of the Alliance Store, with a double barreled shotgun in his hands, which was suddenly jerked out of his hands by masked men. The mob then rushed in, yelling "Throw up your hands or we'll blow your brains out", and instructing the guards to tie up the prisoners. Steward's estimate was "a hundred or more". Huse Holmes agrees that the orders were to tie the prisoners, then the mob "armed them" out the door.

It must be stated at this time that both William Monroe Evans and his son John Henry Evans were known criminals, and much feared by those unfortunate enough to find themselves at their mercy, of which there was very little!

When the mob entered, it was with no thought of hanging the father-son duo. Remember the Guntersville Democrat article about them whipping a man almost to death? I am convinced that this was to be "pay-back" time, as I believe that whipping victim was a member of the "White Caps!"

When the mob entered, William Monroe Evans, with a flourish of the arrogance in which his life was cloaked, said "Give me my riding whip and I'll whip this whole crowd!" as he reached out and unmasked one or more of the members. Although I am sure the Evans pair would have spent some very uncomfortable time that night being flogged, I believe William Monroe Evans committed what might very well be described as suicide with that show of bravado, as he recognized the unmasked face or faces, and the mob knew that if William Monroe and John Henry Evans lived, then those revealed to them were dead men, who would be tortured into identifying the others before they were killed, so they could be dealt with by the gang one at a time! This was the Evans gang's way.

An alternative story: William Monroe Evans, rather than removing the mask from the mob members, just started to recognize members by their mannerisms, voices, etc. and began calling them by name, with a little too much accuracy for the future safety of those being called. That is when the options dwindled away, and death of the Evanses became necessary.

"Mun" and John could not comprehend that they were in danger, such was their contempt for their fellow men, their neighbors!

The bound prisoners were taken from the Alliance Store in a generally Southerly direction (perpendicular to Highway 69) down past the Baileyton school, then a turn to the right, along the road past the Baileyton cemetery, all the way to the end of that road, then turned right again, traveling that road back toward Baileyton for about seventy-five to a hundred yards, then going to an old hickory tree maybe ten yards to the left of that road, which was to be the final stop of their lives for William Monroe Evans and his son John. There is a lesser road turning off that road just past where the tree stood.

The mob, to look for proof of it's intentions, had not brought a rope! If I intended to hang two people, I would have brought along enough rope to hang two people with a rope each, probably using a drop from the back of a horse to break their necks, in a somewhat humane way of executing them. Well, I don't have much doubt that the mob was as smart as I am, and here they are without a rope, yet ready to hang two men!

While the main body of the mob was proceeding from the store to the tree, a conference was held by the leadership of the mob, and the decision was made to hang both father and son. William Monroe was known for what he was, a bullying desperado who would unhesitatingly kill anyone who crossed him. It was felt by some that John Henry was worse than his father, snakelike, with no conscience whatsoever. His record, although short, was filled with crimes, such as the shooting from ambush of Pierce Mooney, then threatening the life of Dr. G.W. McClarty in an attempt to prevent his treating Mooney for his wound inflicted by John Henry Evans.

The decision was made by the leadership of the mob to hang the pair, and a runner was sent back to the Alliance store for rope. Unfortunately, there wasn't much rope left on the roll there! The runner took it all, and went to overtake the mob and prisoners, finding them at the aforementioned hickory tree.

The rope was described to me by Charles J. Humphries in a videotaped interview as being of manila, or hemp, commonly known as "sea grass" rope, about a half to three quarters inch in diameter. The rope was reported to me to still, to this day, remain in the possession of the Guthrie family. Charles told me he had seen the rope, but I have not.

Only upon the arrival of the messenger with the rope did the pair start to realize their plight! Without more than the necessary delay, they were affixed, one to either end of the rope, which had been passed over a limb of the hickory tree. This precluded any possibility of dropping the prisoners' weight to break their necks, instead they were doomed more or less to die of a garrote smothering, or deprivation of oxygen, rather than a true hanging, with snapped spines.

When this message became clear to the hapless souls, the bluster and bravado were gone, they pleaded for their lives (as I'm sure I would have done for mine) but there was no turning back without sacrificing the member or members recognized by both father and son. The identified members would have died, by whatever torture necessary to make them reveal any other names of mob members they knew. The die was cast!

Although seeming barbaric, an attempt was made at a humane approach to ease the choking process. The younger members of the mob rode their horses at full speed toward the hanging men, and leaped off their horses to clutch the bodies around the waist with their arms, similar to bulldogging a steer in modern rodeo, adding their weight and momentum to the hanging body, to break their necks and end their suffering. While this was still rather brutal, remember that these people had never hanged any- one before. They had practically no time for plan- ning, and simply did the best they could in a trying situation.

Tales would be told to families, other tales would be told to law enforcement agencies, but much of the truth now is buried without ever being revealed to anyone. The investigation that followed, complete with rewards offered, was some kind of a tribute to the brotherhood that existed within the mob. Folklore says there was never anyone prosecuted in connection with it. That is not quite accurate, as we shall see later.

With the deed done past any reversal, the mob rather quickly faded away from the old hickory tree, with it's grim burdens swinging gently in the summer breeze. The members of the mob were on their way home to face that first of many nights they would spend wide awake, staring at the ceiling.

The Evanses were on their way to their final resting place, in the family burial plot known as the "Evans Graveyard" on a hill above "The Falls", which much later became the "Welcome Falls".

The old cemetery was revisited by the author and others during the research for this book.

Arvel Holcomb, Charles J. Humphries, Joan Mims, Norris Evans, and his wife Bobbie Evans. This picture taken in May, 1993 at the scene of the old Evans Cemetery, near "Welcome Falls". It is now in pasture, but it was in the days of my youth in a cultivated field, under a scrub cedar tree.

Suspended Sentence Chapter Six

The aftermath

The people of the community knew what was coming, but did they really? This was the only lynching ever recorded in Cullman County, and it was two white men, neither of them tried for nor convicted of any major crime. Very early it became apparent there would be the Devil to pay!

The following is the way the Alabama Tribune broke the news to the world on the following Thursday, when the weekly newspaper was next printed after the lynching.

The Alabama Tribune, August 20, 1891

THE HANGING OF W. M. AND JOHN EVANS

Wm. Monroe Evans and his son John Evans were citizens of Morgan County, near the Cullman County line. They were men not held in high esteem by many of the best citizens of their neighborhood. By many they were considered dissolute and dangerous.

Of late, several crimes have been committed in the neighborhood, which from circumstances and threats have been laid at their door. About the first of June, one Pierce Mooney, while at work at home, was shot from ambush and dangerously wounded. Other parties at whom the Evans had a grudge have been shot, and they were suspicioned of doing the shooting. Many expressed themselves as being afraid of being ambushed and killed.

On last Thursday, John Evans was arrested on a

warrant sworn out before Justice Heaton for the shooting of Mooney, who lives in this county. He was carried to Baileyton for trial. From some cause, satisfactory to the Justice, the trial was postponed until Monday. In the meantime Monroe Evans went over to Baileyton to see and assist his son in his trial, and before getting off his horse he was arrested and put under guard.

(This doesn't seem like much time to prepare for trial, but things were done that way then, with no more than the absolutely necessary delay. After the fanfare of the recent O.J. Simpson trial, it seems more like a good idea, doesn't it?)

The following article is from the Alabama Tribune. The Guntersville Democrat, Huntsville Gazette, and other newspapers also made contributions toward informing the public at that time, and so help to inform us today, as well.

On August 16th, an inquest was held into the deaths of William Monroe Evans and his son John Henry Evans in the Baileyton School, which had been turned into a makeshift morgue. The Tribune account of this inquest follows:

State of Alabama, Cullman County

This is to certify that the following named householders of the County Cullman was impaneled and sworn to hold inquest on the bodies of W.M. and John Evans on the 16th of August, 1891, at Baileyton in Beat 13:

Jury: J.A. (Jonas) Donaldson, John Mitchell,

W.M. Pate, H.H. Young, J.M. Gill, J.W. Burden, and G.W. McClarty, M.D.

Baileyton, Alabama August 16, 1891. I, one of the jury impaneled and physician, hereby certify that on post mortem examination of the bodies of W.M. and John Evans, it was found that their necks were broken or dislocated from hanging by a rope across a limb which produced death.

G.W. McClarty, M.D.

Witnesses:

J.H. Holmes (*James Huston Holmes*): About 11 o'clock, the time they came in I was lying on the counter at the lower end of the store asleep. The prisoners, W.M. and J.H. Evans, were asleep when I lay down-both up the left hand counter. When I awoke, the house was about half full of men and all well armed and they ordered me to throw up my hands. The orders were to tie them, then they armed them out-and not open the door in half an hour and they left a guard at the door on the outside. All the men were masked and supposed to be about fifty or sixty, or perhaps one hundred.

G.C. Steward: I was sitting in the door at the Alliance Store with a double barrel shotgun in my hands. The first thing I knew my gun was jerked out of my hands by masked men and they ran in the house saying "throw up your hands or we will blow your brains out-go forward and tie them up." They tied W.M. and John Evans, then the house was so crowded with men I did not see what became of the prisoners. The crowd then passed out and ordered us to lock the door for half an hour or they would shoot our brains out. They left a guard outside. There were a hundred men or more.

S.T. Fleming, J.A. Hendrix, and D.E. Dendy, hearing the evidence of G.C. Steward, indorses (sic) the same.

E.S. Steward-I was a guard but not on duty. I was out at Mr. Holmes' (James Huston) resting. I was aroused by men passing in the direction of the Alliance Store and I ran out and they halted me and carried me with them near the store and stopped and kept me there some twenty minutes while they were getting the prisoners from the storehouse. Then they said for me to go back to bed. I suppose there were about 200 men. They were all masked, wearing white caps, and afoot.

Mr. J.B. "Joe" Gober who was in hearing of the above evidence as well as C.B. Brandley (*actually Columbus Bradley*) indorsed (sic) the same.

Verdict of the jury: We, the jury, impaneled by J.M. Heaton, J.H. Stevens, and I.C. Oaks, all of whom are acting Justices of the Peace for said county, after inspecting the bodies of W.M. and John Evans and hearing the evidence of all the guards, we find that on the night of the 15th last between the hours of 10 and 12 o'clock P.M. the said W.M. and John Evans came to their deaths by the hands of a body of masked men by being hung to the limb of a tree and their necks broken.

(*, Some of this material is repetitive, but it appeared as noted in the various articles*)

The newspaper articles were fairly numerous, but often saying very little that could be called specific. One article, entitled "A Black Day at Baileyton" says "On Thursday, August 13, 1891, Justice of the Peace J. Matt Heaton arrested 21-year-old John Evans (actually he was 25) on a warrant sworn out by Pierce Mooney. He was placed in jail at the Alliance Store at Baileyton and guards were posted. The following day, his father, Monroe Evans, was arrested and placed in jail with his son. On Saturday, an angry mob overpowered the guards, removed the prisoners from the jail and hung them on a tree limb.

If these men were guilty of any crime they were entitled to a fair trial and punishment according to the law. The unfortunate affair is to be regretted and will be condemned by all good citizens. Efforts will be made to bring all who participated in the tragedy to justice.

The following material is from accounts published in the Alabama Tribune and other sources at the time of the lynching. It is here through the courtesy of Margaret Jean Jones.

On last Thursday *(13 Aug 1891)* John Evans was arrested on a warrant sworn out before Justice Heaton for the shooting of Mooney, who lives in this county. He was carried to Baileyton for trial. From some cause, satisfactory to the Justice, the trial was postponed until Monday. In the meantime, Monroe Evans went over to Baileyton to see and assist his son in his trial. Before getting off his horse he was arrested and both put under guard.

Why they were not permitted to give bail or sent to the county jail for safe keeping, we have never learned, and seems to be the only cause for censure against the officials who had them in charge. Knowing the citizens of Baileyton and the surrounding county as we do, we are loth (sic) to believe they would willingly participate in a crime that would bring trouble upon them or disgrace to their community. If these men were guilty of any crime they were entitled to a fair trial and punishment according to the law. The unfortunate affair is to be regretted and will be condemned by all good citizens. Efforts will be made to bring all who participated in the tragedy to justice. Other noteworthy comments and facts follow:

We, the citizens of Baileyton and vicinity deeply deploring the course pursued by the mob, availed themselves *(ourselves?)* of the first opportunity to get a full attendance and called a citizen meeting in the Alliance Hall at 5 o'clock P.M. August 21. J.H. Hamilton was called to the chair and T.B. Hodge was appointed secretary.

At this meeting a resolution was adopted which "deeply deplored the awful deaths of the Evans men and pledging to use all means in the bounds of prudence and desecration *(discretion?)* to bring such criminals to justice and to put the officers of the law in possession of any facts relating to the case that may come into our possession." The resolution was signed by 120 citizens.

One article reads "According to old-timers in the area, it is not believed that anyone was ever arrested in the case, although several have maintained knowledge of deathbed confessions".

A Letter to the Editor of the Alabama Tribune

The *(Birmingham)* Age Herald's correspondent, writing under date of August 17, gave only part of the facts, and they were misleading.

In the reference to the shooting of Mooney last May, he says "No suspicion at the time rested against anyone."

In this he erred, for Mooney and his friends had little doubt as to the guilt of some member of the Evans family having done it. Threats had been made and these and the guilt of her son are now virtually sustained by the confession of Mrs. Evans. *(The confession mentioned is not available to the author, probably lost forever).*

Again, the correspondent says that after John Evans' arrest "He repeatedly asked to be allowed to make bail but was refused. Neither would they allow anyone to speak to him."

The facts are that the Magistrate did not think he had jurisdiction over the case and sent to town to inquire of Judge Hays and to ask him to set bond. Furthermore, the Evans were both allowed to speak freely with friends in private, or secret, until indirect threats and implications were made to one of the guards by one of the Evans party. The action of the Evans party on the ground led the guards to believe that there was trouble brewing and that an effort would be made to overpower the guards and release the prisoners during the night. The known character of the Evans family strengthened such belief.

The guards were almost totally unarmed. The mysterious and threatening manner of the Evans party having excited apprehension, prudence dictated that the guards prepare for emergency. Hence, "Men were out around the place as far as five miles on Saturday night, ostensibly *("Ostensibly" is an interesting choice of a word*) borrowing guns to guard the prisoners." John Evans' trial was not set for Saturday. Before the arrest of Monroe he asked the Justice to set the trial for 10 o'clock Monday that he might have time to secure counsel. His request was granted. They never asked to be allowed to waive examination and give bond for their appearance at Circuit Court. The guards nor their friends did not apprehend a lynching and their precaution was to protect themselves from the opposite direction.

Citizen

In September, 1891, a group of people met with the County Commissioners of Cullman to request that they post a $200.00 reward for revelation of persons involved, with an extra $100.00 added if the accused were jailed.

The following article seems to have been written at a much later date. It is by the courtesy of Margaret Jean Jones, appearing in her historical book "Combing Cullman County."

August 15, 1891 was a black day in the history of Baileyton, and it's terrible events have become a legend passed on to each new generation. It was on this hot Saturday night that Monroe Evans and his son John were hung in what is believed to be the only lynching ever to occur in Cullman County.

According to legend, the Evans men, who lived just across the line in Morgan County, were notorious outlaws. During the Civil War, Monroe Evans, who had many enemies, is said to have sought revenge by joining a band of Union soldiers headed by John Dickey. The group rode over North Alabama plundering households, killing old men, and abusing women.

When a crime wave, the exact nature of which is not known, hit Baileyton in 1891, Monroe Evans and his 20 year old son were blamed. Following a direct accusation by Pierce Mooney and the Goodlett brothers, Monroe and John Evans shot Pierce Mooney in the back *(actually in the leg, per my best information)* as he worked at home in June, 1891. A month later they threatened the doctor (G.W. McClarty) who was attending Mooney.

Pierce Mooney promptly swore out an arrest warrant for John Evans, but Justice of the Peace Matt Heaton was obliged to wait until the Evans men returned to Cullman County to make the arrest

(*No jurisdiction in Morgan County*). On August 13, Constable Heaton and the Goodlett brothers were warned that the (*Evans*) pair were on their way to kill the Goodletts.

Constable Heaton intercepted Evans on the road and arrested him peacefully with the intention of calling an immediate trial. Evans demanded a lawyer and was placed under guard in the Alliance Store until one could be contacted. Upon learning of his son's arrest, Monroe Evans came to investigate. Feelings were beginning to run high, and the older Evans was placed under arrest even before he dismounted from his horse. Heaton ordered a heavy guard placed around the makeshift jail.

Word of the arrests spread quickly to surrounding communities, and by nightfall on the fateful day a masked and angry mob had converged on Baileyton. The guards were overpowered and the prisoners taken to a spot about one-half mile South of the Alliance Store *(this was also the old Masonic Hall building)*.

Some old-timers insist that the original intention was to whip the men, but when they recognized some of the mob ringleaders it was decided to hang them on the spot. A rope was thrown across a tree limb and father and son died facing each other.

Monroe Evans' last words were said to be "Lord, have mercy, boys. I ain't done nothin'."

The bodies swung from midnight until 4 P.M. on Sunday when they were taken down and placed in a temporary morgue in the schoolhouse. According to the late J.H. Guthrie, whose sister Belle was born on the night of the hanging, the Evans men were buried on the A.M. Holcomb farm on Route 1, Baileyton, just across the line in Morgan County.

Rewards were offered for information but no arrests were ever made in the case. Several deathbed confessions are said to have been made years later.

(There are numerous errors in the preceding article, such as the age and arrest of John Evans)

The next day, Monday, August 17th, 1891, their two man coffin was finished by Miles Humphries and family, with his wife and other female relatives doing the interior upholstery, and they were placed inside. He was selected to make the coffin because he had a water-powered sawmill located on his farm, giving him a source of lumber. He made most of the coffins for the community at that time.

There was a trip of some five to seven miles to take them back to their home, and then to the Evans Cemetery, which was located on the family farm.

Takers for the job of hauling them that distance were few, considering that they had spent one full day in the Alabama summer sun, then a night and part of another day becoming bloated and odorous, no doubt making the task far from desirable!

On that morning of the 17th, my great grandfather Ephraim Anders Jones hitched his mules to the wagon and went over there after them, hauling them first back to the house, then to the cemetery, where a grave had been dug for them.

One report is that when he arrived at the Evans

Ephraim Anders Jones, great grandfather to the author.

home with the bodies, Mary Polly came out of the house to view the bodies, and when the coffin lid was lifted for her, she lifted the quilt that covered their faces, took a brief look, and turned on her heel, returning to the house without a spoken word. It must have been a horrible sight to look at!

Much of the preceding was told to me by Martha Davis, who was a granddaughter to Ephraim Jones.

The two man coffin must have required several people to unload from the wagon and lower into the double grave, as they were both reputed to be large men.

Although the cemetery is now a long way off the road, across private property there was a road, normally used by the Evanses to intersect the road that passed across the brink of the Falls, passing East of the little knoll where the cemetery was located, within a hundred yards or less, making it possible to drive the wagon right to the cemetery, which would have helped!

I have no insight past that already mentioned as to who dug the grave and buried the bodies.

The following letter is the only material available to so much as mention the childhood and adolescent years of William Monroe Evans, and started out as a building block to construct the history of this lynching around. Unfortunately, there are several issues that don't quite line up with the facts, and it's credibility will have to rest with the judgment of the reader. The same letter appeared in the Alabama Tribune on September 8th, 1891, and on October 8th, 1891, it appeared in the Guntersville Democrat. The only difference in the two copies is the emboldened type, which must have been edited out by the Tribune, but left in by the Democrat. I have combined the headlines.

MONROE EVANS
A True History of his Life and Character
Blue Spring, Morgan County
Sept. 8 and Oct. 8, 1891

Editor; Cullman Tribune *(Guntersville Democrat):*

As some newspapers and their correspondents have had much to say in regard to the lynching of Monroe and John Evans at Baileyton, I think it would be interesting to your readers to know something of the life and true character of Monroe Evans.

It is not my purpose to justify lynch law, or justify men in their action to make lynch law necessary, but our object is to make a true statement as to this man's career, and that justice may be done, "though the Heavens fall." So without the fear of man or the hope of reward we ask space in your columns to give a few facts concerning this man Evans.   We have known Monroe Evans since he was a boy, he being about five years my senior. He lived in Marshall County and I in Madison, about seven miles apart. When a boy he was bigoted, overbearing, and unprincipled, and always engaged in some kind of deviltry.

When the war broke out there lived in the Northern part of Marshall County one John Dickey, a man who was noted for his hatred toward his neighbors and cruelty and brutishness to his wife and children; and when the Federal troops took possession of the country North of the Tennessee River this man Dickey offered his services to the Federal commander who mistook his hatred for his own people for patriotism to the Union, and gave him a commission as captain of scouts with power to organize a company to operate in North Alabama.

Then began a reign of terror. Dickey's company was composed principally of men who had deserted the Confederate army, or had been dodging conscription; and nearly all of them had some old grudge to settle. In this company Monroe Evans was an active member. They were employed as scouts and pilots for the Federal troops, thus giving them a splendid opportunity to wreak their vengeance upon unprotected people. Men were dragged from their homes and murdered, some of them in the presence of their families, by this cruel band of outlaws.

Distinctly do we remember the names of Volney Ellett, Alfred Clark, Davis Russell, Fletcher Lewis, and many others who fell by their hands. Many houses were burned, and many women were thrown out of house and home, without food or shelter, in the midst of winter, for no greater crime than that their fathers, husbands, and brothers were soldiers in the Confederate army.

But the war ended and Dickey and Evans still lived. Dickey went West, but Evans remained in Marshall County, **and married a daughter of Nich. Stevens;** but he could not be idle, he must be about

94

his master's (The Devil's) work. He was soon charged with all manner of crimes, one being taking too many liberties with other people's hogs.

He next organized a clan for self protection, composed of a few white men and several Negroes. They decided they were strong enough to make war on their enemies and made a plot to blow up the Methodist Church and Masonic Hall at New Hope, in Madison County, but the plan leaked out through a Negro belonging to the clan. Warrants were taken out for Evans and his gang and placed in the hands of a deputy sheriff, who summoned a strong posse, your correspondent being one of the number.

The Sheriff moved at once against the band, but they fled to the mountains. After days of hard riding and searching, a part of them were overhauled. They resisted arrest, and firing at once began and six Negroes were killed, or died afterwards from their wounds. Evans escaped though severely wounded. He lay in the mountains until he recovered sufficiently to enable him to travel, when he came to Morgan County. Evans' life in Morgan County has been one of continual lawlessness.

He resided near the Morgan and Cullman County line, on the brink of a mountain, a place well suited to his purposes. He was a Mormon by practice and has raised families by several women besides his own wife. Your correspondent has been reliably informed that this monster in human shape, by continual abuses and by garbled and misquoted extracts from the Bible, he forced his poor ignorant wife to acknowledge that it was right and proper for a man to have as many wives as he wanted.

Nearly every Grand Jury for the last sixteen years have been called upon to remove this blot of corruption and immorality from the community, but Evans, through trained and practiced witnesses who cared nothing more for committing perjury than they did for the wind that blew succeeded in defeating their efforts, and this blot upon Christian civilization remains as an insult to the community and to the dignity of the law. Evans' greatest desire seemed to be for strife, contention, and bloodshed. The shooting of a man several years ago by the Evans that they might further debase his wife is a well-remembered fact in that community. The attempt to assassinate Mooney last spring and the attempt to murder the Goodlett boys is still fresh in the minds of our people, also the oft repeated threats to kill the attending physician of Mooney and Mooney's wife for the attention given Mooney while suffering from his wounds by Evans and his son is a well known fact. It seemed that these inhuman wretches were determined that he should die from neglect if they could not kill him with their bullets.

Monroe Evans only lacked one thing to have made one of the most desperate outlaws in the land, and that was true courage. Rube Burrows was shot down by Carter and his name was lauded to the skies as a hero. Ford, in a most cowardly manner, shot and killed Jesse James but the State of Missouri paid him large sums of money. Both of these men had some redeeming qualities. They were true to their families and true to their friends. But this man had none. He was not true to his country nor his family. But the men who relieved North Alabama of the presence of this man are called by the Cullman correspondent of the Age-Herald "brutes and murderers."

Evans' poor wife is in a better condition. The man who wrecked her life and educated her son for the gallows is gone. She will no longer be insulted by her husband's harem. His gang is scattered to the four winds, and peace and order have taken their place. The last stronghold of the Devil in East Morgan County has been destroyed, and the people say "Amen." Yours for the right,

A.M. Nabors

While this letter gives us information not available from any other source, there are still discrepancies that make it pretty shaky as an authoritative source.

For a man who says that he participated in the *posse comitatus* led by Willis C. Stephens, he certainly came up with a different casualty count than the documentation by the United States Army and Stephens, himself!

He also mentioned this event as a starting point for Mun Evans at avoiding justice, said string of years totaling sixteen per Nabors, which would place the point sixteen years before Evans' death in 1891, or 1875. Actually the incident at Wild Goat Cove took place in 1869!

The shot which struck Mun's arm became a major life threatening wound in the above letter, and the move that was made to Morgan County after this still left Mun and family in Marshall County for the 1880 census, so I'm not quite sure when that move was made, nor how complete the move was!

Does the pursuit lasting for days sound anything like the trip to L.A. Bronson's place told about by Stephens and others? Why didn't someone else mention the six Negroes who were killed on the spot or later died of their wounds? I am still looking for answers to those questions, and wondering if Nabors really was there!

Of course in the interest of fairness, he could have been the only one telling the truth about this whole affair! You can judge that one for yourself!

The Baileyton Alliance Store, where the prisoners were held by the law until taken by the mob. The second floor held the Masonic Lodge hall.

Suspended Sentence Chapter Seven
The decision

The Farmer's Alliance was a cooperative venture owned by the people it served, occupying the first floor of the building. It was also a farmer's union, drawing some harsh criticism from other farmers, who obviously were not members in newspapers of that era!

The second floor of the building known as the Baileyton Alliance Store housed the Masonic Hall. A picture of the original Alliance Store is presented herein similar to the way it looked at the time of the lynching. The actual building has been gone for many years, and has been replaced by a combination gas station-party store.

The roads are still laid out pretty much the same as they were then, with the road going past the East side of the store, going generally South past the school. A road turns right off that road, going generally West, alongside and past the Baileyton Cemetery until it intersects with another road, with an angle greater than ninety degrees, and heading generally North, back toward Baileyton.

Along this road, they traveled North for fifty to one hundred yards, until they reached a large hickory tree on the left, or West side of the road, where the work of the mob reached it's conclusion on that night of August 15th, 1891!

If one looks at the route they traveled, it quickly becomes apparent that they didn't have a clear destination when they began the trip with the prisoners from the Alliance Store. It would have been much nearer to just take the latter road out of Baileyton, almost straight South to the tree.

Common sense tells you that they weren't particularly interested in a moonlight stroll with the prisoners, they were just more or less stalling for time while the leadership of the mob modified the decision to horse-whip them into one to hang them!

The decision went from a horse-whipping in retaliation for that beating administered to a White Cap member, as mentioned by the Guntersville Democrat, to hanging, in the interest of self-preservation after William Monroe's display of bravado arrogance leading to his learning the identity of one or more mob members. Had the Evanses not died, those members of the mob so recognized were as good as dead men!

They would have been taken by the Evanses and their gang at a time and place of their choosing, and tortured until they revealed the names of all other mob members they knew. This torture might well have included the brutalization of their families as well.

Now if you were a member of that gathering that night, what would you have done? These people were not vagabonds and drifters, they were the heart of the citizenry of Baileyton and environs, with wives, children, property, and roots in the soil of Baileyton and the surrounding area. As such a member, you have the loyal obligation to protect the members of your group who were recognized by the father-son duo, and now where is the nearest thing to the road of prudence left available to you?

This question was answered differently by different people after the fact, in the light of day, but to their credit, they stood by their friends and fellow members that night.

The next step was to send a runner back to the Alliance Store for rope to carry out the sentence. If you were planning to hang someone, wouldn't you have brought along enough rope to hang them separately, with enough rope to drop them from the back of a horse so their necks would break, or some such equivalent? I would have, and they were probably as smart as I, likely even more so. But here they were, without a rope!

To further complicate matters, when the runner returned with the rope, there hadn't been enough on the roll of rope in the store, and it became necessary to hang them on opposite ends of the same rope, to hang there for a garrote strangling rather than a true hanging.

A humane attempt was made to shorten this process, with the younger men riding their horses at top speed toward them, leaping off their horses as they threw their arms around their bodies, lending their own weight and velocity to the breaking of their necks. It is doubtful if it helped much, if any! They had probably already died before this could be started.

It wasn't an easy task, with the bluster and bravado displayed by both William Monroe Evans and John Henry Evans. They had ridden roughshod over anyone and everyone who had stood in their path until they could not conceive of anyone, or for that matter, any group or mob, having the intestinal fortitude to make them pay the ultimate price for the threat they posed to those identified members.

Picture the burden placed on the shoulders of every member or person in attendance that fateful night! Many of them lived to be old men, but they were mostly young men at that time, and would carry that burden to their graves. There is a lot of difference in horse-whipping someone who richly deserves it in your honestly considered opinion, and hanging them to a tree with less than enough rope, to hang there and choke before your very eyes, as you try the "bulldogging" technique in a probably vain attempt to shorten their agony.

In my investigation and consideration of all I could learn about this affair, I have concluded that William Monroe Evans and his son John Henry Evans not only were not the only losers on this night, they probably were not even the greatest losers.

After this night, the Evanses would suffer no more, but the dawn would make hunted animals out of the perpetrators, even though none but the group of which they were participants knew of their involvement, could you trust *all* of them? Remember, it only took the failure of one knowledgeable person, turning State's evidence, to put them all on the gallows, or into prison for the rest of their natural lives! In the eyes of the law, this could hardly be considered anything less than first degree murder!

Can you picture what your life would become instantly? You would have to wear the burden well, or you would give yourself away! The approach of a stranger would strike terror to your heart, but you must not flinch! Not only for a few days, but for the rest of your life, as there is no statute of limitations on murder!

Equally burdensome is the knowledge that if you make one slip at the wrong time, to the wrong person, you have not only brought your own house of cards crashing down, you have brought your trusted, and trusting, friends down with you!

The threat wasn't long in materializing, as Governor Thomas Jones seemed to take it personally that they had taken prisoners from the protection of the law in Alabama and hanged them, and a rather large task force of Alabama's best detectives were placed on the case, with budgeting to keep them going as long as necessary. This probably became the most intensive and prolonged man hunt in the history of Alabama!

Wherever you looked you might behold someone asking questions about yourself or others, looking over your shoulder, or asking questions of your friends, making you wonder how your friends were answering said questions, and as time passed, the detectives were asking more and more knowledgeable and pointed questions, making the participants aware that someone was giving them information, and that the noose was gradually tightening around the group who had taken the lives of William Monroe and John Henry Evans there at Baileyton that night in August, 1891.

The constant fear of them all was that someone was talking too much, and the detectives seemed to be getting more and more information from *somewhere!*

They were telling the people who were suspected about the merits of telling all to save their own skins by turning State's evidence, and telling them that it really didn't matter whether they did or not, as they already had enough evidence to convict all of those suspected, anyhow!

The psychological drain must have been tremendous, soon making you afraid to say "good morning" to anyone, lest you give away secrets or damaging information.

The burden would grow heavier with time, and trust would start to fade between the participants, as detectives no doubt told them that their friends had already talked and told them everything, probably even giving examples of information they had received, with the participants knowing full well that the source of such information had to have been someone in attendance at the hanging to possess such knowledge!

Can you picture the terrible toll this situation would take from families? How much did they dare talk with their wives, lest a loose tongue should prove the undoing of them all? I'll bet it was difficult being the child of someone carrying such a burden, as that would probably generate a lot of irritability as well.

As the threat continued the weight on their shoulders increased also, becoming overpowering, to the point that those in it's focus became more and more desperate, and at some time it must have come home to all that they were trapped, and the claustrophobic nightmare must have become too heavy to bear, giving one the urge to leap out of a sleepless bed to scream as loud as you could to the entire world *anything* that might bring an end to this hideous nightmare once and for all!

To look at this situation from the viewpoint of the detectives, it must have been a very challenging as well as personally rewarding case as they extracted both information and documented proof over a period of almost four years from some *very* reluctant people.

Their philosophy was based upon the inescapable fact that the patience of the predator is greater than that of the prey, hence the cat will patiently wait until the mouse runs out of patience, and then it's mealtime! This is Nature's way, as cats have to eat, too!

The detectives first sowed seeds of doubt among their targets, then patiently maintained the pressure and took up every little bit of slack as it was given to them for the three plus years between the lynching and the trial.

The maneuvering by both sides must have put a checker or chess game to shame while it lasted over those three years!

Many of the less prominent parties involved left the country, those who had no property or families holding them in the area suddenly felt other places calling to them from afar!

Two of my great uncles, William Thomas "Uncle Tommy" Holmes, and James Harrison Jones "Uncle Jim" left the country during this period, going, according to all I have been able to learn, to Texas. I have not been able to pick either of them up there in the records. It is possible they might have changed their names. William Thomas Holmes and James Harrison Jones both stayed wherever it was that they went, never returning to Alabama. However, James Harrison Jones' wife Martha "Mattie" Durham did return in about 1920. I have a picture taken of her by Martha Davis, her niece, at that time!

William Thomas Holmes married Desa Mahaley Evaline Anderson. They left two children buried in the Lawrence Cove Cemetery, Morgan County, Alabama, and never returned to visit the graves.

His brother, my grandfather Benjamin Franklin Holmes left an unfinished letter to him when he died in 1935. My aunt, Bessie Florence Holmes, finished the letter, mailed it, and continued to correspond with "Uncle Tommy" until his own death in 1938. Unfortunately, I don't know where he was at the time!

According to Mabel (Holmes) Burks, her "Uncle Huse" (James Huston) Holmes built a house at Joppa, and built it so there was not a room in it without an outside door! I suspect this might have been an example, or symptom of the paranoia created by the lynching and following activity! Incidentally, he was the first Mayor of Joppa, as well.

Although it is far beyond the scope of this book, it would be interesting to see some of the marks that affair left on people, and how they were affected by the residue it left behind!

Suspended Sentence Chapter Eight
Lightning bolt!

This is the Cullman County Court House where the trial was held. This building was heavily damaged by fire in 1912, but it is claimed no records were lost, although some were damaged by water.

Suddenly the worst possible event had come to pass! The morning of November 24th, 1894 was bad news to those participants who had been badgered and persecuted by detectives for the intervening years and months between the lynching of William Monroe and John Henry Evans and this date. There would be some raised eyebrows in Cullman County this day!

The detectives assigned by Governor Thomas Jones to investigate this case had done their work, and done it well! It is unfortunate that they must remain anonymous, but I have found no record of their identity! It had been predicted by most knowledgeable people that they would come up empty, with no indictments, no substantiated accusations. *This was far from the truth!*

New Sensation in Alabama
Alabama Tribune, 22 Nov 1894
Prominent citizens arrested for lynching the Evans brothers in 1891! (*They were father and son, not brothers*)

John and Monroe Evans were lynched in this county in 1891. The Governor and this county offered a reward for the lynchers. Twelve men accused of complicity in the crime have just been arrested and are in jail here. Many others are yet to be arrested. One of the County Commissioners is among the accused, and is in jail. The evidence is said to be strong against all of them. They are from the Eastern part of the County. The United States indicted the other gang from the Western end of the County. (*This leaves an unanswered question, I have been unable to find any other reference to this second gang, from the Western end of the County)*

Alabama Tribune, 29 Nov 1894
Indictment
State of Alabama, Cullman County
   The Grand Jury of said County charge that before the finding of an indictment, John Goodlett, Ben Goodlett, Tom Entrican, Joseph Gober, Huse Holmes, Joseph Keller, Louis Keller, Ben Donaldson, Jonas Donaldson, John Humphrie, Andrew J. Cash, Columbus Bradley, Jim Cottle, and William P. Turner unlawfully, and with malice aforethought did kill John Evans by hanging him with a rope.
   And the Grand Jury further charge that John Goodlett, Ben Goodlett, Tom Entrican, Joseph Gober, Huse Holmes, Joseph Keller, Louis Keller, Ben Donaldson, Jonas Donaldson, John Humphrie, Andrew J. Cash, Columbus Bradley, Jim Cottle, and William P. Turner unlawfully and with malice aforethought did kill John Evans by placing a rope around his neck and drawing him by said rope up off the ground by means of drawing said rope over the limb of a tree, thereby strangling said Evans to death.
   (By way of explanation, the last paragraph doesn't seem to be correct, even as detailed as it is! Actually, it seems to me that the rope was placed over the limb, and one Evans was attached to each end of it! Likely it was tied around the neck of one, then thrown over the limb with a turn around the limb, and the other was then attached to the opposite

110

end!)

And the Grand Jury of said county further charge that John Goodlett, Ben Goodlett, Tom Entrican, Joseph Keller, Louis Keller, Ben Donaldson, Jonas Donaldson, John Humphrie, Andrew J. Cash, Columbus Bradley, Jim Cottle, and William P. Turner unlawfully and with malice aforethought did kill John Evans by placing a rope around his neck, drawing said rope over the limb of a tree, thereby suspending the said John Evans off the ground, and in such a position jerked him and pulled him and broke his neck.

And the Grand Jury of said county further charge that John Goodlett, Ben Goodlett, Tom Entrican, Joseph Gober, Huse Holmes, Joseph Keller, Louis Keller, Ben Donaldson, Jonas Donaldson, John Humphrie, Andrew J. Cash, Columbus Bradley, Jim Cottle, and William P. Turner unlawfully and with malice aforethought killed John Evans by tying a rope around his neck and drawing said rope across the limb of a tree, thereby suspending the body of said John Evans off the ground with his hands tied behind him and kept him so suspended and helpless until he was dead against the peace and dignity of the State of Alabama.

William H. Sawtelle
Solicitor of the Eighth Judicial Circuit

Circuit Court Docket, (Same date)
No. 660 (Case Number)
State of Alabama,

Cullman County

The State vs. John Goodlett, Ben Goodlett, Tom Entrican, Joseph Gober, Huse Holmes, Joseph Keller, Louis Keller, et als.

Indictment for Murder
(No Prosecutor)

(The following consist in part of those who turned State's evidence. Why Turner and Entrican aren't mentioned is a mystery beyond my comprehension!)

Witnesses:

D.W. Draper, A.J. Cash, Columbus Bradley, Molley Evans, Frank Mooney, Rody C. Widner, J.M. Heaton, Jerry Martin, Luther Holder, Till Mooney, Joe Wheeler, and John Widner.

(James Matthew "J.M." Heaton was the Justice of the Peace who arrested Mun Evans before he dismounted from his horse in Baileyton, and was most probably the Cullman County officer who hand carried the papers to Marshall County, presented them to the authorities there, and took custody from the Marshall County Sheriff Wells of John Evans after the arrest, then took him back to Baileyton to stand trial.

It was difficult to get the county sheriff to even appear in remote locations in the county due to the slow transportation of the time, so much of the law enforcement work was done by local justices of the peace in their own communities.)

A True Bill:

A.J. York, foreman of Grand Jury.

Presented in open court to the presiding judge, by the foreman of the Grand Jury, in the presence of all other Grand Jurors,

(signed)
Charles Grafton, Clerk

The State of Alabama
Cullman County

I, Charles Grafton, clerk of the Circuit Court, in and for the said county, do hereby certify that the within and foregoing is a full and complete and correct copy of the original indictment found by the Grand Jury of said county against the within named persons.

Witness this 27th day of November, 1894.
Charles Grafton, Clerk

Alabama Tribune Dec. 17, 1894 (repeated January 10, 1895)

A special term of the Circuit Court will be held beginning Jan 28, 1895, State of Alabama, Cullman County.

Office of Clerk of the Circuit Court
To All Whom it May Concern:

Take notice that by order of Hon. H.C. Speake, Judge of the 8th Judicial Circuit, a special term of the Circuit Court will be held for said County of

Cullman to commence on the 4th Monday, the 28th of January, 1895, for the disposal of State cases only, and by further order of Hon. H.C. Speake all witnesses in criminal cases now on the docket will be subpoenaed to appear at the first day of said special term. Defendants will take notice, and govern themselves accordingly.

This December 24th, 1895 (actually 1894).

Charles J. Grafton, clerk
Alabama Tribune Dec. 17, 1894
(Repeated January 10, 1895)

It is pretty difficult to picture a court being alive and functional on Christmas Eve in today's world, no matter what the urgency or provocation, isn't it?

(This doesn't remind one too much of the O.J. Simpson fiasco, does it? This two week time limit came very near being too short, having this case result in a mistrial, by the time a jury was selected and testimony taken, followed by deliberations by the jury)

List of Jurors for Special Term
Alabama Tribune, Jan. 28, 1895
First Week:

William Guthrie	Henry N. Stricklin
George W. Hinkle	James M. Rogers
Joseph G. Pope	John J. Whitehead
Dennis Doyd, Jr. (Boyd?)	Joseph A. Baver
F. W .H. Speegle	James G. Clayton
F. H.Hayes	A. E. Karter
S. S. Leeman	E.W. Harper

John S. York	Riley Maze
A. F. Carmichael	L. S. Long
W. M. Kinney	Gus Neubaur
W. H. Sizemore	James T. Raney
A. T. Tanner	James T. Anderson

Second Week

John C. Roberts	J. H. Chatin
John W. Giles	Lord B. McAdams
Marion W. Pierce	Joseph G. Otto
G. W. Shed	D. H. Howell
Hiram L. Pollard	James H. Murphee
Arthur J. Viek	William H. Oden
J. D. Small	S. J. Calvert
R. V.Kelley	W. T. James
Samuel L. Aldridge	J. A. McMinn
David G. Burks	David J. Dodson
Elijah J. Smith	William J. Burks
William A. Chance	

EVANS

Alabama Tribune, Thursday, Jan. 31, 1895

Despite the inclemency of the weather, the intense popular interest in the famous Evans murder case brought out an immense crowd at the opening session. Routine work of organization consumed Monday afternoon's and Tuesday morning's sessions.

Apparently the weather was pretty extreme, but the people were undaunted by it, turning out in large numbers for the trial. Can you imagine a trial in Cullman, Alabama at that time when about two hundred witnesses "answered to their names"? The jury pool was rather large as well, but still they were unable to seat a jury without calling a few others after the pool was exhausted! It must have been difficult to find a place to park your team and wagon. No doubt McEntyre's hitch lot must have been overflowing!

I am sure there couldn't have been sufficient lodging available for so many people, so it seems likely that they must have camped out in that bad weather just to attend that trial!

It attracts a lot of attention to see a dozen of your top status citizens fighting for their lives in the county's courts.

Thursday, Feb. 7, 1895
Circuit Court Docket

Case #660, State vs. John Goodlett and others, murder of John and Monroe Evans set for trial Thursday, 31st inst.

Thursday, Feb. 7, 1895
The case of the State vs. John Goodlett and seven others, indicted for the murder of John Evans, was called for trial Thursday Morning last, and has since been in progress.

Finis Ewing St. John was one of the prosecuting attorneys in the case. He was the second St. John in the Alabama Legislature, and the first of at least four carrying the name Finis Ewing St. John. (*photo courtesy Margaret Jean Jones)*

(The Alabama Tribune was published on Thursdays, and there was apparently no thought of publishing an extra edition, news just had to wait until Thursday to be published!)

The Alabama Tribune
January 24, 1895
Circuit Court Docket

Case #660, State vs. John Goodlett and others, murder of John and Monroe Evans set for trial Thursday, 31st inst.

Thursday, Feb. 7, 1895

The case of the State vs. John Goodlett and seven others, indicted for the murder of John Evans, was called for trial Thursday morning last, and has since been in progress.

The work of impaneling a jury consumed all of Thursday, but nine being selected out of a special venire of 72. Friday morning a jury was completed consisting of the following persons:
L.T. Lay, S.T. Tanner, W.M. Quattlebaum, T.A. Glasscock, W.B. Wade, Jas. T. Scott, William B. Scott, L.M. McPherson, George A. Bailey, John Yielding, B.F. Still, and R.G. Oden. At the calling of witnesses, about two hundred responded to their names.

Friday, Saturday, and Monday were spent in the examination of State witnesses, the most important of whom were Cash, Enterkin, Turner, and Bradley, parties who had turned State's evidence in the case. Tuesday morning the defense began it's testimony, aiming to impeach the State's witnesses to that effect.

As Court will adjourn Saturday night, it is at present doubtful if any conclusion in the case will be reached this Court. Joe Keller, Houston Holmes, Jim Cottle, and Louis Keller were arrested, charged with the crime, and brought to Cullman and lodged in jail. The arrest was made on the basis of evidence furnished by A.J. Cash and three other parties, who were alleged accomplices, but turned State's evidence.

A special term of Court to try the case was set for Jan. 28, and on the first day of Court the case was called and set for trial Thursday, Jan. 31st.

Tuesday morning the defense began it's testimony. The plan of defense counsel was to establish the character of the defendants, and to impeach the State's witnesses. Quite a horde of witnesses to this effect were introduced, all telling the same story without exception.

After concluding the taking of testimony able arguments for the State were made by Messrs. F.E. St. John, S.I. Fuller, and W.T. Sawtelle, and for the defense by Messrs. W.T.L. Cofer, Jessie Brown, and L.C. Dickey. Saturday morning the case was given to the jury, who weighed the merits of the case, and finding that there was not, to their minds, proof of guilt beyond a reasonable doubt, soon brought in a verdict of not guilty of the charge of killing John Evans.

They were released from jail Saturday afternoon,

and permitted to once more return to their homes.

(Author's note: There are many diverse spellings of the names cited herein, with no sure way to arrive at the correct spelling by any other method than the one used here, which was to use the spelling used in the article from which the information came.)

The case of the State vs. John Goodlett and seven others, indicted for the murder of John Evans, was called for trial Thursday morning last, and has since been in session.

Thursday, Feb. 14, 1895

The White Cap Case

On Saturday morning, Aug. 16, 1891, in the Eastern part of the county, the lifeless forms of two persons who had been hanged to a tree during the previous night were found. Who were the perpetrators of the awful deed still remains a mystery.

Rumors afloat soon gave out the information that the murderous work was done by an organized band of "WHITE-CAPPERS" belonging to the vicinity of Baileyton. Shrewd detectives were put on the case, and no effort was spared to secure the arrest and punishment of the guilty parties. but all efforts were fruitless until the autumn of 1894 when John Goodlett, Bill *(Ben)* Goodlett, Ben Donaldson, Jonas Donaldson, Joe Keller, Houston Holmes, Jim Cottle, and Louis Keller were arrested, charged with the crime, and brought to Cullman and lodged in jail. The arrest was made on the basis of evidence furnished by A.J. Cash and three other parties, who were alleged accomplices, but turned State's evidence.

A special term of Court to try the case was set for Jan. 28, and on the first day of Court the case was called and set for trial Thursday, Jan. 31st.

More than a day was consumed in securing a jury, whose names were given in our last issue. Friday morning taking of testimony for the State was begun, and lasted until Monday night. Several unimportant witnesses were examined, but the sensational testimony was brought out when Cash was put on the stand. In his testimony Cash told of the workings of an organized band of so-called White-Cappers, and how the hanging was planned and executed by the defendants.

His story was told in a very straight-forward manner, and he endured a remarkably severe cross-examination. His story was largely corroborated by those belonging to the vicinity of Baileyton.

Friday, Saturday, and Monday were spent in the examination of State witnesses, the most important of whom were Cash, Enterkin, Turner, and Bradley, parties who had turned State's evidence in the case.

As Court will adjourn Saturday night, it is at present doubtful if any conclusion in the case will be reached by this Court.

This was followed by the last meaningful newspaper article in the series, with this one being from the Guntersville Democrat, dated February 14th, 1895. It pertained to the preceding Saturday, February 9th, when the verdict was actually reached, but the paper was not published until the following Thursday. Note that it falls short of literary excellence where the names are concerned, as many of them are either misspelled or the wrong names in the first place!

"WHITECAPPERS ACQUITTED"

The famous Evans Whitecap trial has ended, and a verdict of "Not Guilty" has been rendered by the jury. So it goes abroad that the defendants, Houston Holmes, Joe Gober, Ben Donaldson, Jonas Donaldson, James Coddell, Dr. Lewis Keller, John Goodlett, and Dan Goodlett are not the men who killed John Evans on the 15th of August, 1891.

It has been a long trial and an interesting case. Both sides fought to the best of their ability, but the defendants have come out free as to the charge.

The same charge stands against the defendants for the murder of Monroe Evans and the defendants will have to remain in jail until they can either be released on bail or stand trial for the offence. It is thought they will be permitted to give bond and go home to their families and await the regular session of the court for the next trial.

Thus ends the first, last, and only trial held for the Evans lynching at Baileyton, Alabama on August 15th, 1891. They did post bond and go home until the State decided to Nol Proseque (non prosecute) their case. While the names are spelled badly, and even the wrong names used, it is apparent who they were referring to in this article.

Now people involved, along with their families, could begin to pick up the pieces and start putting their lives back together.

It is hard to measure the impact this event had on the lives of so many! As a result, many people were born in a different location, married in a different location, and died in a different location.

The ripples from that explosion are still around, with people still wondering why their ancestors moved from one location to another.

I have looked diligently for my two great-uncles, William Thomas Holmes and James Harrison Jones, who left the country to avoid prosecution, in my opinion. Did they go to Texas and change their names? How many others were even born under a different surname as a result of that lynching?

This kind of thinking is enough to boggle one's mind, and many people will never understand the hand of fate working to alter their lives even before they were born!

Suspended Sentence Chapter Ten
Documentation and records

First we will deal with some of the charges against William Monroe Evans. This information is in limited supply, but it pretty clearly establishes the life style and character of William Monroe Evans!

The following material, while sometimes closely resembling some previous entries, is different, in that it came from the actual cursive script court records rather than the newspapers. Much of the following wasn't believed to exist, and had eluded researchers for a hundred years. I was lucky, plus I had some very competent help from Carolina Nigg in locating the documents, but the bad news is that alongside this material were several empty folders, suggesting that the remainder of the documents were at some time in the past relegated to the garbage can as worthless waste paper!

I will title each item, all parenthetical notes are mine where I feel clarification may be necessary, or where the information may be incomplete.

Monroe Evans Indictment

The State of Alabama vs. Monroe Evans

No. 267 C.P.C.

For Indictment record in this case see Indictment Record page 28.

The State of Alabama, Cullman County

(*The above mentioned indictment record not available*)

To any Sheriff of the State of Alabama Greeting:

124

An Indictment having been found against Monroe Evans at the Spring term 1886 of the Circuit Court of Cullman County for the offense of carrying a pistol concealed about his person.

You are therefore commanded forthwith to arrest said defendant and to commit him to jail, unless he give bail to answer such indictment at the present term of our Circuit Court now in session in said County and make return of the writ, according to law. Witness my hand this 30th day of April, 1886.

Julius Damus, Clerk of Circuit Court

Executed by arresting the within named defendant and bringing him in Court.

(signed) A.J. York, Sheriff

Minute of entries:
The State of Alabama C.P.C. No. 267 vs. Monroe Evans

On the 30th day of April, 1886, comes the State by Robert W. Bell, Solicitor pro tem and the defendant in person. And the defendant in open court consents that the indictment may be amended by striking out William Evans and inserting Monroe Evans, his true name. And therefrom the defendant with Seaborn S. Dagnell and Daniel M. Gilmore in open court agree to pay the State of Alabama Two Hundred Dollars for the use of Cullman County, unless the defendant appear at this term of this court, and from term to term, and day to day thereafter until discharged by law to answer a criminal prosecution for carrying a pistol concealed about his person, and in favor thereof said defendant and bail waive the right of exemption as to personal property under the Constitution and Laws of the State of Alabama.

(The above exemption refers to the State exemption applying to personal property, that the State couldn't take away below a certain minimum. This exemption was waived by the said bondsmen)

The State of Alabama
No. 267 vs. Monroe Evans

Indictment for carrying a pistol concealed. On this 17th day of November, 1886, comes the State by John Turrentine, Solicitor pro tem, and the defendant in person and by attorney. And the defendant being arraigned in open Court, upon hearing the bill of indictment in this case read, pleads "Not Guilty" thereto.

And therefore comes a jury of good and lawful men to wit: Joseph Fromhold, and eleven others, who being duly elected, impaneled, sworn, and charged according to law upon their oaths do say: "We, the Jury find the defendant not guilty." It is therefore considered by the Court that the defendant be discharged from this prosecution and go hence without day (*delay?*).

The above is one of the few cases found on record against William Monroe Evans. While I have a strong suspicion there were many others, they have disappeared from the files, leaving a few cases basically intact, such as the preceding, and fragments of others, such as a bail bond for appearance that is very strongly evident in a mortgage referring to court appearances.

The following is somewhat vague, but I am reporting the evidence as I have it, not as I wish it was.

The State of Alabama
No. 334 vs. A & B
Monroe Evans alias Monro Ivens

On this 27th day of November, 1888, comes the State by H.C. Jones, it's Solicitor, and the defendant in person and by attorney. And the defendant demurs to the second count of the Indictment on file in this case., which demurrer is sustained by the Court and the defendant being arraigned in open Court.

Upon hearing the bill of Indictment read in this case, pleads "Guilty" to the other Counts of said Indictment, and upon motion of the Solicitor and the defendant agreeing thereto, it is considered by the Court that the fine against said defendant be paid at the sum of one cent. Thereupon the defendant, with S.L. Fuller and J.R. Freeman, confess judgment as provided by law for said fine of one cent and the cost of this prosecution and in favor thereof, waive by an instrument in writing their rights to all exemptions of personal property under the constitution and laws of the State of Alabama. It is therefore considered by the Court that the State of Alabama, for the use of Cullman County have, and recover a Judgment against the defendant and S.S. Fuller and J.R. Freeman for said fine of one cent and the cost of this prosecution, for which let execution issue, and against this judgment and the execution and other process to issued thereon, there is no exemption of personal property of the defendant and his sureties.

(The above is all of the information available on this case. While the fine of one cent might seem trifling, when coupled with the "costs of prosecution" it was probably a fairly impressive sum of money at that time, in that economy.)

Now let us turn the coin over, and look at some of the handwritten Court records pertaining to the indictments, prosecution, and bail bonds of those charged with the murder of the Evanses. Some of the other people indicted but not tried would have no doubt gone to trial had the initial trial resulted in convictions, but since they couldn't convict the leaders, even with the four perpetrators turning State's evidence, they prudently gave up on what might well be called the "lesser fish".

Indictment
John Holmes, Bob Biggers, and Jim McCleskey
(There are identical individual indictment records for the three mentioned here, and in order to avoid needless repetition, I will print it once, with the three names.)
The State of Alabama, Cullman County Circuit Court, Fall Term A.D. 1894.

The Grand Jury of said County charge that before the finding of this indictment John Holmes, Bob Biggers, and Jim McCleskey unlawfully, and with malice aforethought did kill Monroe Evans alias Mun Evans by hanging him by the neck with a rope, and the Grand Jury of said county further charge that John Holmes, Bob Biggers, and Jim McCleskey unlawfully, and with malice aforethought did kill Monroe Evans alias Mun Evans by placing a rope around his neck and drawing him by said rope up off the ground by means of drawing said rope over the limb of a tree, thereby strangling said Monroe Evans alias Mun Evans to death.

And the Grand Jury of said County further charge that John Holmes, Bob Biggers, and Jim McCleskey unlawfully, and with malice aforethought killed Monroe Evans alias Mun Evans by placing a rope around his neck, drawing said rope over the limb of a tree, thereby suspending the said Monroe Evans alias Mun Evans off the ground and in such position jerked and pulled him and broke his neck, and the Grand Jury of said County further charge that John Holmes, Bob Biggers, and Jim McCleskey unlawfully, and with malice aforethought killed Monroe Evans alias Mun Evans by tying a rope around his neck and drawing said rope across the limb of a tree, thereby suspending the body of the said Monroe Evans alias Mun Evans off the ground, with his hands tied behind him, and kept him so suspended and helpless until he was dead.

(signed)

W.H. Sawtelle
Solicitor of the 8th Judicial Circuit
Filed in open Court this 28th day of November, 1894
(signed)
Chas. Grafton, Clerk

A Warrant for John Holmes:
(*Other warrants were not available*)
The State of Alabama, Cullman County Circuit Court.
To any Sheriff of the State of Alabama Greeting:

An Indictment having been found against John Holmes at the fall term 1894 of the Circuit Court of Cullman County for the offense of killing Monroe alias Mun Evans and John Evans.

You are therefore commanded forthwith to arrest said John Holmes and commit him to Jail to answer such indictment at the next term of our Circuit Court, to be holden (held?) for said County on the first Monday in May next, and make return of this writ according to law.

Witness my hand, this 12th day of December, 1894.

(signed) Charles Grafton, Clerk
(This John Holmes is a great uncle of the author)

The State No. 668 vs. John Holmes
Indictment for the murder of John Evans
On this 9th day of Feb. 1895 comes the State by it's Solicitor and the defendant in his own proper

130

person and by attorney and on motion and sufficient cause shown it is ordered by the Court that the defendant be admitted to bail in the sum of Fifteen Hundred Dollars.

Thereupon comes the defendant John Holmes with W.A. Childers, J.M. Grant, I.C. Oaks, and M.L. Self and agree to pay the State of Alabama the sum of Fifteen Hundred Dollars, unless the said John Holmes appears at the next term of the Circuit Court and from day to day and from term to term thereafter until discharged by law to answer a criminal prosecution for the offense of Murder.

(W.A. Childers was for more than twenty-five years pastor of Harmony Church, located in Lawrence Cove. J.M. Grant was his brother-in-law, while I.C. Oaks was a Justice of the Peace who sat on the inquest held over the bodies of William Monroe Evans and John Henry Evans on August 16th, 1891 in Baileyton, Alabama. I was not aware they were all acquainted with each other)

The State No. 669 vs. John Holmes
Indictment for the Murder of Monroe Evans

On this 9th day of Feb. 1895 comes the State by it's Solicitor and the defendant in his own proper person and by attorneys and on motion and sufficient cause shown it is ordered by the Court that the defendant by admitted to bail in the sum of One Thousand Dollars. Thereupon comes the said defendant John Holmes with W.A. Childers, J.M. Grant, I.C. Oaks, and M.L. Self and agree to pay the State of Alabama One Thousand Dollars unless the said John Holmes appears at the next term of the Circuit Court and from day to day and from term to term thereafter until discharged by law to answer a Criminal prosecution for Murder.

This is the story of John Holmes in the court records, as he was charged and bailed out on said charge. He never went to trial.

This seems to conclude the case of John Holmes. Nol Proseque is an agreement by the State to not prosecute the case. This might indicate that he, being less important than some other participants, might not have been worth moving his records to another location, such as the archives in Georgia. I simply don't know what happened with the other records!

We now begin the saga of the others making bail, and it is interesting to note who some of the bail bondsmen were, for which defendants. A little more information, where available, will be given under "Participants", later in the story.

The State No. 669 vs. John Goodlett, et als.
Indictment, Murder of John Evans
On this 23rd day of Sept. 1895 comes the Solicitor who prosecutes for the State and all the defendants in their own proper persons and by attorneys and on motion it is ordered that a Nol Proseque be entered in this case to which said order the defen-

dants **object and except.**

(The ending phrase of this declaration, although used often, is not clear to me, but it looks like a misuse of words by the clerk. I don't think the defendants objected to being released on bond. The word "except" should probably be "accept", which I'm sure they did!)

Next we will deal with the bail bonds, and the bondsmen who stood as surety for the defendants. In some cases they are very interesting connections, or associations. They knew people I never even suspected that they might have known. To place one's property, both real and personal, in a position of possible forfeit for a person requires more than a passing acquaintance with a person! The following defendants posting bond are the eight defendants who actually stood trial, after the other four, namely Andrew Jackson Cash, Tom Enterkin *sometimes spelled Entrican, or Entrekin*, William P. Turner, and Columbus Bradley, opted to turn State's evidence to avoid prosecution.

The State of Alabama No. 667 vs. John Goodlett, Ben Goodlett, Tom Enterkin, Joseph Gober, Huse Holmes, Louis Keller, Ben Donaldson, Andrew J. Cash, Columbus Bradley, Jim Cottle, and W.P. Turner.

Indictment, Murder of Monroe Evans, alias Mun Evans

On this the 9th day of February, 1895, by order of the Court the following named defendants were admitted to Bail in the sum of twenty five hundred Dollars, to wit:

John Goodlett, Ben Goodlett, (Tom Enterkin, lined out), Joseph Gober, Huse Holmes, Louis Keller, Ben Donaldson, Jones Donaldson, and Jim Cottle.

Thereupon comes into Court John Goodlett and also F.A. Moore, I.C. Oaks, D.W. Draper, G.W. McCormick, and W.G. Holmes. And agree to pay the State of Alabama twenty five hundred Dollars unless the said John Goodlett appears at the next term of this (Court?) and from day to day and from term to term thereafter until discharged by law to answer a criminal prosecution for the offense of the murder of Monroe Evans.

Also comes into open Court the defendant Ben Goodlett with S.W. Biggers, D.W. Draper, A.M. Nabors, and James A. Stewart and agree to pay the State of Alabama twenty five hundred Dollars unless the said Ben Goodlett appears at the next term of the Circuit Court and from day to day and from term to term thereafter until discharged by law to answer criminal prosecution for the murder of Monroe Evans.

Also appears into open Court the defendant J.B. Gober with T.T. Dickerson, I.G. Albritten, J.K.P. Bryan, G.W. McClarty, and W.R. Lowery and agree to pay the State of Alabama the sum of twenty five hundred Dollars unless the said J.B. Gober appears at the next term of the Circuit Court and from day to day and from term to term thereafter until discharged by law to answer a criminal prosecution for the murder of Monroe Evans.

Also appears in open Court the defendant Huse Holmes with J.L. Roberts, J.B. Sherrill, and B.F. Holmes and agree to pay the State of Alabama twenty five hundred Dollars unless the said Huse Holmes appears at the next term of the Circuit Court and from day to day and from term to term thereafter until discharged by law to answer a criminal prosecution for the offense of murder of Monroe Evans.

Also comes into open Court Louis Keller with A.J. McClarty, R. Bowden, and G.W. Peck and agree to pay the State of Alabama the sum of twenty five hundred Dollars unless the said Louis Keller appears at the next term of the Circuit Court and from day to day and from term to term thereafter to answer a criminal prosecution for the murder of Monroe Evans.

Also comes into open Court the defendant Ben Donaldson with J.A. Donaldson, D.W. Draper, W.G. Kelly, and G.W. McClarty and agree to pay the State of Alabama the sum of twenty five hundred Dollars unless the said Ben Donaldson appears at the next term of the Circuit Court and from day to day and from term to term thereafter until discharged by law to answer a criminal prosecution for the offense of murder of Monroe Evans.

pp221 Circuit Court minutes Feb. 9th, 1895 Special term 1895

Also appears in open Court the defendant Jones

Donaldson with E.W. Christian, J.A. *(John A.)* Donaldson, and R. Bowden and agree to pay the State of Alabama twenty five hundred Dollars unless the said Jones Donaldson appears at the next term of the Circuit Court and from day to day and from term to term thereafter until discharged by law, to answer a criminal prosecution for the offense of murder of Monroe Evans.

Also appears in open Court Jim Cottle with P.W. Wiley, T.M. Cottle, G.M. Robertson F.N. Henderson and J.H. Stephens and agree to pay the State of Alabama the sum of twenty five hundred Dollars unless the said Jim Cottle appears at the next term of the Circuit Court and from day to day and from term to term thereafter until discharged by law to answer a criminal prosecution for the offense of murder of Monroe Evans.

It is further ordered by the Court that the defendant Josiah Keller be admitted to bond in the sum of one thousand Dollars. Thereupon comes the defendant Josiah Keller with A.J. McCarley, G.W. McClarty, W.C. Winn, M.T. Self, and A.E. Drichel and agree to pay the State of Alabama the sum of one thousand Dollars unless the said Josiah Keller appears at the next term of the Circuit Court and from day to day and from term to term until discharged by law to answer a criminal prosecution for the offense of murder of Monroe Evans.

Indictment, Murder of John Evans
The State vs. No. 665 Josiah Keller
On this the 9th day of February, 1895, comes the

State by it's Solicitor and the defendant in his own proper person and by attorneys and it is ordered by this Court that the defendant be admitted to bail in the sum of fifteen hundred Dollars.

Thereupon comes the defendant Josiah Keller, A.J. McCarley, W.C. Winn, M.T. Self, and A.E. Drishel, and agree to pay the State of Alabama fifteen hundred Dollars unless the said Josiah Keller appear at the next term of this Circuit Court and from day to day and from term to term thereafter until discharged by law to answer a criminal prosecution for the offense of murder of John Evans.

(Although these bonds don't seem like much when compared to present day bail bonds, we are talking about a time when William Monroe Evans put up one hundred sixty acres of land and considerable livestock to secure a loan for one hundred twenty-five dollars. These bonds were quite a lot of money to raise at that time in that place!)

The bondsmen were numerous and varied, but in general consisted of the wealthier farmers, for more or less obvious reasons. It must have been pretty hard for those people to place their farms and property at risk to gain the freedom of their friends and relatives, but none remained in jail for lack of a posted bond!

Note that none of them jumped bond, either, which must have been quite a temptation, just to escape from a situation which must have looked rather bleak!

Benjamin Franklin Holmes, who acted as bondsman for his brother and no doubt attended the trial was grandfather to the author. He never mentioned having any knowledge whatsoever to my mother and her siblings throughout the rest of his life!

Suspended Sentence Chapter Eleven
Further documentation

The following is from the Court minutes. Some of them are simply not available, but this particular entry is revealing as to the jury selection procedure, also telling us of other people involved at the time and in that place in the trial.

Circuit Court Minutes
Jan. 28th, 1895 Special Term 1895
Jury No. 1

William Guthery	Henry N. Stricklin
Geo M.Winkle	James M. Rogers
Joseph G. Pope	John G.Whithead
Devis Loyd, Jr.	Joseph A. Bovar
S.S. Leiman	E.W. Harper
John S. York	A.F. Carmichael

The following named persons were duly elected and empannelled as Jury No. 2, to wit:

L. T. Lay	Wm. Kinney Gurtan
Neubauer	W.H. Sizemore
James S. Raney	James T. Anderson
S.T. Tanner	Henry Stalimer
W.W. Quattlebaum	F.M. Holmes
W.B. Wade	Travis T.Glasscock

And the Court now being fully organized, the following proceedings were had:

It appearing to the satisfaction of the Court that A.E. Karter had been duly summoned to appear at the special term of Court and serve as a Petit Juror and the said A.E. Karter failing to appear it is ordered by the Court that a Secire Facie be served on said A.E. Karter, to appear at the next term of this Court and show cause why a Judgment of Contempt should not be entered against said defaulting juror.

It is ordered by the Court that all depositions filed in Criminal Cases be opened.

The State of Alabama No. 660 vs.
John Goodlett, Ben Goodlett, Tom Enterkin, Joseph Gober, Huse Holmes, Louis Keller, Ben Donaldson, Jones Donaldson, A.J. Cash, Columbus Bradley, Jim Cottle, and W.P. Turner: **Indictment, Murder of John Evans**.

On this, the 28th day of January, 1895 comes the Solicitor who prosecutes for the State and the defendants in their own proper persons and by attorneys, and on Motion of defendants John Goodlett, Ben Goodlett, Joseph Gober, and Jim Cottle it is ordered by the Court that the Order of Severance made at the fall term 1994 of this Court be set aside, and said John Goodlett, Ben Goodlett, Joseph Gober, and Judge agree in open Court to a jurist trial with Huse Holmes, Louis Keller, Ben Donaldson, and Jones Donaldson embraced in said indictment.

This separation had the prosecutors feeling like they were in "Hog Heaven", with the defendants standing ready to destroy each other, until Leonidas C. Dickey, the high priced "Hired Gun" attorney arrived on the case. This was one of the first things he accomplished, the re-uniting of the defendants. It was a brilliant move, but I'll bet some of the defendants took some convincing!

It is further ordered by the Court that the trial of this case begin Thursday, the 31st of January, 1895. Thereupon, the Court caused the Box containing the names of the Jurors of the County to be brought into Open Court and having the same well shaken and the defendants being present in Open Court the presiding Judge then and there drew from said box the name of the following fifty jurors, to wit:

Name	Beat
1. John Sutterer	1
2. Daniel M. Winkle	16
3. W.B. Scott	4
4. Martin Burkhard	10
5. W.T. Self	3
6. L.M. McPherson	16
7. S.H. Herrin	1
8. D.P. Davis	1
9. Chas R. Harris	4
10. John Schwan	5
11. T.M. Tucker	6
12. W. R. Stricklin	6
13. W.F. Holmes	11
14. H.M. Stricklin	15
15. Hill Harbison	6

16. G.C. Glasscock	2
17. Francis M. Patrick	11
18. Hazel A. Young	13
19. John O. Holland	9
20. Jas. T. Scott	4
21. W.B. Lott	6
22. S.S. Thornton	2
23. T.M. Landers	4
24. John H. Screws	14
25. J.M. Tucker	6
26. T.J. Culpepper	6
27. W.L. Dahlke	1
28. David J. Gentry	8
29. Elbert C. Hicks	8
30. C.B. Wilhite	10
31. S.T. Box	12
32. H.M. Burkhard	10
33. John H. Arwood	1
34. W.A. Taylor	4
35. John Kesler	1
36. W.T. Tillery	10
37. T.K. Speegle	5
38. D.P. Florence	15
39. W.L. Brown	5
40. James H. Wallace	1
41. G.W. Cone	16
42. F.B. Blalock	4
43. G.S. Collins	5
44. Martin L. Drake	11
45. Pinkney Elliot	4
46. T.J. Rushing	6

47. Isaac James, Jr.	7
48. George A. Bailey	3
49. Thomas Guthery	5
50. Elijah Knight	4

The list of which was immediately made out by the Clerk of the Court and it is ordered by the Court that the Clerk of this Court furnish the Sheriff of this County with a Vinire of said so drawn Jurors and the Sheriff is ordered to summon said Jurors to appear in Court on the 31st day of January, 1895, it being the day set for the trial of this case. It is further ordered by the Court that the Jurors so drawn as aforesaid, together with the regular organized Pannel (sic) of Jurors, empannelled for the present week of the term shall constitute the Pannel from which the Jury to try this case shall be selected. It is further ordered by the Court that the Sheriff shall personally serve upon each of the defendants, at least one entire day before the day set for trial of this case, a certified copy of the list of the regular organized pannel of Jurors subponaed for the week of this term of Court and the Special Jurors drawn as aforesaid. And it is further ordered by the Court that attachments be issued for Mary Evans, Ol Roberts, Rhoda C. Widner, and Jos. Widner to Morgan County and for Howell Adams and Till Mooney to Marshall County, for John Giles to Cullman County, and West Sanders to Madison County returnable on Thursday, January 31st, 1895. Thereupon, the Court adjourned until 9 o'clock tomorrow morning.

This is the only mention I have found of Mary Evans, who had apparently returned to Marshall County after the death of William Monroe Evans.

The Evans property was bought by Jesse Van Holcomb and his wife Mary Elizabeth (Slaton) Holcomb apparently pretty shortly after the Evans' death. I am not knowledgeable of whether the sale was direct. I don't know if she re-established relations with the Nicholas Stephens family or not. She is still a somewhat unknown entity at that time in her life!

Fourth Day, Jan 31st, 1895

Court met pursuant to adjournment at 9 o'clock A.M. Robert J. Fuller, Sheriff, returned into open Court the special Venire Facie heretofore to wit: Issued to him on the 29th day of January 1895 on which said Venire is the following return to wit: In pursuance of the within Mandate of the within writ, I have executed the same by summoning, as directed in said writ all persons named therein except D.P. Davis, John Schwan, G.W. Cone, T.M. Tucker, and John C. Holland, who were not found.

No. 660 The State vs. John Goodlett, Ben Goodlett, Joseph Gober, Huse Holmes, Louis Keller, Ben Donaldson, Jonas Donaldson, and Jim Cottle. *(Joe Keller is missing)*

Indictment: Murder of John Evans, continued from page 209. On this the 31st day of January,

144

1895, comes the State by it's solicitor W.G. Sawtelle and the defendants in their own proper person and by attorneys, and defendants. by leave of Court defendants interpose a demurrer filed on Jan. 31st which being considered by the Court is overruled, thereupon defendants withdraw their plea of not guilty and move the Court to quash the Venire of the Petit Jury on the grounds set out in said motion, which being duly considered by the Court is over-ruled, and the defendants except .

Thereupon, the State by it's solicitor and the defendants by their attorneys select the jury to try this case, and L.T. Lay, S.T. Tanner, W.W. Quattle-baum, W.B. Wade, W.B. Scott, L.M. McPherson, Jas. T. Scott, Travis A. Glasscock, and George A. Bailey were selected and the jury not being complete and the panel of regularly organized jury for this week together with the panel of the specially drawn jurors being exhausted it was ordered by the Court that the Sheriff summon six qualified citizens of this county to be and appear in Court on the morning of Feb. 1st, 1895, of whom to complete the jury to try this case, and it appears to the satisfaction of the Court that W.L. Brown, and Isaac James, Jr. have been duly summoned as special drawn jurors to appear in Court on this day, and they having failed to appear it is ordered by the Court that Secire Facie be served on the said W.L. Brown and Isaac James, Jr. requiring them to appear at the next term of this Court and show why a Judgment of contempt should not be entered against them. D.L. Sims being duly sworn by the Court as Bailiff the above nine selected jury men as part of the jury to try this case were given in said Bailiff's charge.

Thereupon, the Court adjourned until 9 o'clock A.M. tomorrow.

Circuit Court Minutes Feb, 1st. 1895 Spring Term 1895
Fifth Day, Feb. 1st. 1895

Court met pursuant to adjournment at 9 oclock A.M.

The State of Alabama No. 660 vs. John Goodlett, Ben Goodlett, Tom Enterkin, A.J. Cash, Joseph Gober, Huse Holmes, Louis Keller, Ben Donaldson, Columbus Bradley, Jones Donaldson, Jim Cottle, and Wm. P. Turner. *(Note the absence of Joseph, or Josiah, Keller)*

On this, the 1st. day of Feb. 1895 come into open Court John Gerdes, C.F. Stewart, Peter Winkelbach, Tandy Gray, Leroy McEntire, and Max Schmitt, parties who had been summoned by the sheriff of this county per order of the Court on January 31st. 1895 of whom to complete the jury to try this case, and none of the above named persons being chosen as jurors, it is ordered by the Court to summon six more qualified citizens of this county of whom to complete this jury. The Sheriff summoned J.V. Stallings, B.F. Still, F. Krelhans, G.W. Hancock, John Yielding, and W. Mager, of whom B.F. Still and John Yielding were selected to serve as jurors in this case. And the Jury being still incomplete the

146

Court ordered the Sheriff (*to summon?*) two more qualified citizens of this county of whom to complete this jury.

And the Sheriff summoned F.T. Morris and R.G. Oden, and of whom R.G. Oden was selected. The jury now being complete the said defendants John Goodlett, Ben Goodlett, Joseph Gober, Huse Holmes, Louis Keller, Ben Donaldson, Jonas Donaldson, and Jim Cottle were again arraigned and hearing the indictment read to them again, each of the said defendants and separately plead "Not Guilty" thereto.

And during the progress of this trial on Motion of the Solicitor it is ordered that a Nol Pros (*Non Prosecution agreement by the State*) be entered against the defendants Tom Enterkin, Andrew J. Cash, Columbus Bradley, and Wm. P. Turner et als (?). (*this was their reward for turning State's evidence*)

And on the 9th day of Feb. 1895 after hearing all of the testimony in this case and hearing the argument of Counsel of the State as well as for the defendants, comes a Jury of good and lawful men to wit: John Yielding and eleven others, who having been duly elected and empannelled, sworn, and charged according to law upon their oath do say Not Guilty as charged in this indictment and it is ordered that they go hence discharged by law in this case.

This, then, is the final result of the only trial ever held over events occurring on that historic night of

August 15th, 1891 near Baileyton, Alabama, County of Cullman, when the lynch mob gave William Monroe Evans and his son John Henry Evans a "Suspended Sentence!"

Although it has been over a century since it happened, I am sure the facts of that matter still wield a profound effect on the lives of many people in this nation, born, married, or buried elsewhere because of migration induced by this matter, for instance, and a host of other things that influenced the lives of many people around Baileyton, as well.

Walter Bell Dickey, son of John C. Dickey. John C. and his son Walter Bell Dickey are buried in the New Hope Cemetery, New Hope, Alabama. Picture through the courtesy of Jack Dickey.

This Cullman County Court House replaced the one that was destroyed by explosion and fire in 1912. This one served Cullman County from 1913 to 1965. They stood on the same site.

Benjamin Franklin Holmes

This is my maternal grandfather, and a brother to John S. and James Huston Holmes, as well as William Thomas Holmes, who heard Texas calling sometime between 1891 and 1895, believed by the author to have been involved in that affair. He was a bondsman for his brothers, and no doubt attended the trial in Cullman County in 1895, but the subject was never discussed in the presence of my mother and her siblings.

There is no indication that B. F. was involved in any way in the lynching that I have been able to find.

Joseph Heinchie and Elizabeth "Lizzie" Andrews Creel Heinchie was notified on the day of August 15, 1891, that something was scheduled to happen. Nobody in the family knew what was told to him, but he didn't go, instead he spent a sleepless night pacing the floor. Obviously his worst fears were well grounded!

The old log cabin still stands on the Miles Humphries place after all of these years. This was at one time the "kitchen" for the much more impressive two-story house which stood in front of it, but it served as the home of Eldred Humphries, father of Miles.

This is also the site of the wedding of James Huston Holmes' wedding to Ann Humphries, sister to Miles.

I have been inside the old cabin, but the interior is gutted, with the mantel over the fireplace now being on the back porch!

Ora (Keller) Holmes, daughter of Dr. L. M. Keller and Jane (Box) Keller, wife of Archie Bethel Holmes, born 21 August 1897.
She will turn 100 years as of August 21, this year of 1997!

Dr. Louis Montiville Keller

Dr. Keller is the only person I know to have been in atten-
dance at the lynching on August 15th, 1891 of whom I have
been able to acquire a picture.

One rumor I have heard is that he was there to perform
surgical castration on the Evenses, as punishment for past sex
crimes and prevention of future ones.

Things got out of hand, with Mun recognising too many
members of the mob, and the party turned sinister, resulting
in their deaths.

Buford Burks, Mabel (Holmes) Burks, and Dr. Murray, a business associ-ate, in 1961. This is the lady who was helpful beyond words, telling me about conversations and events that were recorded nowhere else except in her agile mind!

Mabel is the daughter of Anderson Miller Bailey Holmes, known as "Anse Holmes" She is the niece of John S. Holmes, James Huston Holmes, Benjamin Franklin Holmes (my grandfather) and William Thomas Holmes, who left Alabama for Texas between 1891 and 1895. I have not been able to pick up any trace of him in Texas, leaving me to wonder if he might have changed his name!

She is also a granddaughter of Jacob Henderson Holmes.

Ephraim Anders Jones was the father of Frances Josephine (Jones) (Durham) Holmes. He was born 12 January 1844, died 26 April 1923, and rests in Etha Cemetery, Cullman County, Alabama beside his second wife Saphronia Elizabeth (Ransom) Jones, born 25 November 1853, died 5 June 1917. She was a sister to his first wife Mary Matilda (Ransom) Jones, who is buried in Tallapoosa County, Alabama, exact whereabouts unknown.
This is the same Ephraim Jones who hauled the Evans corpses from Baileyton first to the Evans home, then to the family cemetery.

The Cullman County Court House where the trial for the "WhiteCaps" was held for the lynching of William Monroe Evans and his son John Henry Evans.

This building was heavily damaged by explosion and fire in 1912, when records stored therein were damaged by smoke and water, but none were lost, per reports.

This explosion and fire were seen from as far as Joppa, about sixteen or more miles away, by Dr. G. W. McClarty. He might well have been on a house call in the area, as it happened in the wee small hours of the morning.

The reason for the explosion was that the county stored it's dynamite used for road construction in the basement of the court house. I guess we can sasfely assume that practice was discontinued after that.

The Evans Cemetery as it appeared in 1993. The arrows point out the stones that are visible through the weeds. It was formerly in a cultivated field, under a couple of old scrub cedar trees when I was a lad visiting it, and wondering what it was really all about!

The Cast
Part one

The people mentioned in this section are those who made the whole thing happen, whether they were participants at that time and place, or later, in various ways. Some were attorneys, some were bondsmen, some were many other diverse things pertaining to the story. I found them to be part of the story, and they are presented to you in that light.

Just about everyone indicted for the murder of John Henry Evans were also indicted for the murder of William Monroe Evans.

John was no doubt selected for the trial because the prosecutors believed his tender years would arouse sympathy among the jurors, but apparently this was not true! From what I have been able to learn about him, he was a psychopath and a murderer, having no conscience, snakelike, and even worse than his father. He wasn't wise enough to show caution, which no doubt contributed to his downfall as well as to his father's frustration trying to get him out of the messes he got into.

After the acquittal of those charged with the murder of John Henry Evans, the State of Alabama didn't opt for another trial, with it's inherent high price tag, without any real hope for a conviction.

The people who follow played some kind of part in this whole scenario, and will be presented to you to help you understand the event, and also to allow you to meet some of your relatives as I have met mine!

I have employed a technique of presenting pictures of the nearest of kin when I could where the actual pictures were not available. Pictures are rather scarce of those who participated in the "necktie party" after more than one hundred years!

Parenthetical numbers offered are marriage file numbers, to make it easier to secure the actual marriage certificates of your relatives from the court house records if you so desire.

John S. Holmes, who lived from 1851 to 8 Nov 1942, a great uncle of the author and older brother to "Huse" Holmes was indicted but never brought to trial. He first married Catherine W. "Kitty" Lemmons on 20 Dec 1877, by whom he raised his family. Marriage ceremony was performed by William Stringer, Minister of the Gospel. (C2-307)

Martha (Holcomb) Davis can remember going to a singing school at Eva, and stopping by on the way home to visit with Aunt Kitty, describing her as a petite and lovely lady.

His second wife was Eular B (?). He and both wives, along with four of his children are buried in Pleasant Grove Cemetery, near Hulaco, Alabama.

Two of his sons were Elbert and Odie. These children of John were first cousins to my mother. Zular, a daughter, died young, cause unknown. Purley, another son, was killed in a diving accident, his head hitting a submerged rock, per Mabel (Holmes) Burks.

Odie was renowned as a checker player in the Hulaco area, and was also an accomplished pool shooter, and has visited our house on many occasions while selling fruit trees from the Joppa Nursery.

I don't believe I ever saw Odie laugh more than twice in my life, he just didn't do it! He seemed to spend a lot of time in his own world. I can't remember ever meeting Elbert.

John S. was indicted, a warrant issued for his arrest, and he was jailed, making it necessary for him to post bond, but he never went to trial. This was likely because the others who were tried were considered by the prosecution to have played "leadership" roles, or to be easier to convict, or even considered easier to crack and convert to State's evidence witnesses.

One of his bondsmen was his brother Benjamin Franklin Holmes, my grandfather.

After the initial trial, the State decided to "Nol Pros", or non-prosecute the defendants in both murder cases, including those who were tried for the murder of John Henry Evans when it came to the case of William Monroe Evans.

James Huston "Huse" Holmes, 19 Aug 1853/19 Oct 1910, was a great uncle to the author. On 2 Dec 1875 at the residence of E.M. "Miles" Humphries he married Ann Humphries, sister to Miles. This was in Morgan County, Alabama. (C2-193) Huse was probably a "tri-leader", along with Jonas Donaldson and

Dr. Louis M. Keller in modifying the flogging order for the Evanses to hanging after William Monroe Evans discovered the identity of some mob members. *This premise is based at least in part upon their social and economic standing in the community.*

Huse and Ann, along with some of their children, rest in Pleasant Grove Cemetery, along with brother Huse.

Dr. Louis M. Keller, son of Alford Burton Keller, namesake for "Keller Holler", married Jane Box in Blount County, before the county lines changed to their current locations to create Cullman County out of Blount County, Morgan County, and Winston County, on 14 Nov 1872.

I have recently become acquainted with their youngest daughter, Ora (Keller) Holmes, (Mrs. Archie Bethel Holmes). She was born 21 Aug 1897, still living at the time of this writing in 1997.

She told me many things in telephone interviews but her information was second hand, mostly from her mother, as she was only twelve years old at the death of Dr. Keller, and not yet born at the time of the lynching or the trial. She told me that her father continued his practice of medicine, being allowed to leave jail when necessary for that purpose. She told me that her mother would answer any question she asked as openly and as honestly as possible, but with no elaboration whatsoever! This no doubt means she missed a lot of information simply by not knowing which questions to ask!

One of the greatest honors ever bestowed upon me was when I called her on her ninety-ninth birthday, and was invited to attend her one hundredth birthday party! Thanks a lot, Miss Ora, the invitation is greatly appreciated. I will be there if at all possible!

This author did an article appearing in Yesterday's Memories in August, 1996 about Dr. Keller and his daughter Ora.

It is interesting to note that Dr. Keller's son, named William Leonidas Brown "Brown" Keller, born in 1895, the year of the trial, was named for *William* T.L. Cofer, *Leonidas* Cicero Dickey, and Jessie *Brown.* They were the three attorneys making up the defense team, so ably defending those accused in the lynching of John Henry Evans.

My mother and her siblings personally knew Brown Keller. His naming was no doubt a gesture of appreciation by Dr. Keller for the excellent work done by that team.

Ora told me that she attended school in the sixth grade at Eva when the school was located at Gravel Ridge, North of Eva, with Mrs. Jesse Brown as her teacher.

One story I encountered in my investigation was that Dr. Keller was there that night as a physician to perform surgical castration on the Evanses, as punishment for past sex crimes as well as prevention of future ones. This story has it that this was the plan before changing it to hanging. It was also folklore handed down through the descendants of Joe Evans, son of William Monroe Evans. I was unable either to prove or disprove this bit of information.

Dr. Keller was most likely, in my opinion, another tri-leader who participated in the modified decision to hang, rather than whip, William Monroe and John Henry Evans.

The preceding involves some speculation by the author, but has to be somewhere near the truth. Documentation often simply isn't available.

The Cast
Part two

F.E. (Finis Ewing) St. John, the first of at least four by that name, was one of the prosecuting attorneys in the White Cap case. He was the second generation of the St. John family to serve in the Alabama legislature.

He married Miss Nellie Fuller, daughter of Probate Judge and Mrs. Sutton L. Fuller in 1897. He practiced law in Cullman County, Alabama for more than fifty years, during which time he lost both legs to Bright's Disease. He wore the name "The Tall Sycamore".

The name is still around Cullman, I remember a few years ago reading about the death of F.E. St. John IV, and the family was active in Cullman County and Alabama politics during the years of my youth.

Andrew Jackson Cash, the primary State's evidence witness, seemed to disappear from the area, leaving no footprints I can find on his way either in or out of the area.

I can't really say I blame him for leaving the country, as I'm pretty sure he aroused some hostility among his neighbors by turning State's evidence, although I don't know that for sure. I am of the opinion if I had been in his shoes I would have probably have used them for walking elsewhere!

William P. Turner, another one of the four who

turned State's evidence against his fellow partici-
pants, was married to Nancy Angeline Fowler on 23
Aug 1885, ceremony by W.T. Maples, Justice of the
Peace in Morgan County, Alabama. (D-323)

The Turner name is not uncommon in the area of
Baileyton, but it is hard to establish a tie from those
living there today to William P.

Thomas W. Entrekin, another State's evidence
witness, on 20 Dec 1892 married Francis McKissack
(Cullman County Early Marriages). He was a signer
of the petition for the Baileyton Masonic Lodge
#472, dated 3 Mar 1889.

The surname is still available in large numbers in
the area, with spelling variations, but I have no idea
of their relationship to Thomas W. Entrekin, if any.

Columbus Bradley, called at the inquest by the
newspapers by the name "C.B. Brandley" was the
fourth State's evidence witness, and also very little
is known about him, either before or after the events
in question. Again, the far distance seemed to be
calling to at least some of those four as soon as they
could get away after the trial.

J.M. "Johnny" Hendrix, the one tossed across the
road by Ben Donaldson per his own story, lived Mar
1830/Mar 1911, and is buried in Etha Cemetery. His
story sounds almost plausible, but might have been
just more of the cover-up, as he seemed to have been
surprised and not to have   actually known Ben

Donaldson at the time.

The gathering seems to have consisted of men of all ages. Note that he would have been sixty-one years old at the time of the lynching in 1891! Would Ben Donaldson have thrown such an aged individual around like that? Could he have done it without risking serious injury to the older man?

John A. Donaldson, a bondsman for Jonas A. Donaldson, his son, married Martha A. Ryan on 2 May 1854. I believe he was the one known as "Captain Donaldson". An interesting personal note: John A. was the first postmaster at Arkadelphia, Alabama, with the office being named for his wife *Arkadelphia* Ryan.

He was also the first postmaster at Etha, with it being named for his daughter *Etha* Beatrice Donaldson. The Donaldson family burial location is Lawrence's Chapel, where we find John A. and Martha, Beatrice, J.A., Ben, and others of the family.

In the material concerning the founding of Cotaco Post Office, where my grandfather Benjamin Franklin Holmes was post master from circa 1900 to 1907, Etha is mentioned as a neighboring post office "without a public road"!

Cotaco was opened Circa 1893, with Jonathon Pleasant Cobbs as it's master, at the foot of the mountain near the mouth of "Dry Creek" where he built a somewhat ornate two story house that I knew in my youth as the Jonathon Cobbs Place. Jonathon was a first cousin to the Holmes brothers. Their mothers were sisters.

168

Jonathon's son Herbert Dewitt Cobbs, born in 1902, has been quite helpful with background information on people who lived and died before I was old enough to take notice of them. Thanks, Herbert!

About 1900 the office was moved up the mountain past the "Rock Patch" and the old John Ealy Ryan place to the home of my grandfather, Benjamin Franklin Holmes. In 1907, the office moved again, to Eva, Alabama.

Benjamin Franklin was also listed as a bondsman for his brother James Huston Holmes. I have discovered no reason to believe Benjamin Franklin Holmes was involved or present at the lynching, but he was certainly knowledgable of those brought to trial, and no doubt attended the trial.

These facts were never discussed before my mother and her siblings as they were growing up. She told me she had never heard any intimate particulars of the event from anyone! She was not even aware that there had been a trial!

Wm. Ben Donaldson was a man known for his almost super-human strength. He was a very large man, with a brother Luther Donaldson. Luther was a medium to small man, and both wore mustaches.

Bondsmen for Wm. Ben included D.W. Draper, of Lawrence Cove, substantial citizen there as well as post master of Lawrence Cove Post Office. Others were William G. Kelly and G.W. McClarty. W. G. "Bill" Kelly was the father of Lonzo G. "Lon" Kelly, my neighbor whom I remember well! W.G. came to Alabama from the Roopville, Georgia area.

I remember my father and I helping Mr. Lon Kelly butcher a hog when I was probably about seventeen years old. There was no .22 rifle available for dispatching the hog, and we shot it with a 16 gauge shotgun, which he had available.That is the only time I ever even knew of a butchering hog being shot with such a weapon.

The Cast
Part three

Dr. G.W. McClarty was a constantly appearing actor on this stage from beginning to end. He was the physician who conducted the post mortem examination on the bodies of Mun and John Evans, and the one who was threatened by them for treating Pierce Mooney after he was shot by John Evans from ambush while he was working in his blacksmith shop.

He witnessed the explosion and fire of the Cullman County Court House in 1912, from Joppa, some 16 miles away. He might well have been on his way to or from a house call, as it happened in the wee small hours of the morning.

Mrs. G.W. McClarty rests in Pleasant Grove Cemetery, but the location of his interment is unknown. I believe G.W. was a son of S.V. McClarty, although I am not sure.

Jonas A. Donaldson, or "Jones" Donaldson as he was often called by the newspapers and court records, as well as his friends, was the County Commissioner referred to in the Alabama Tribune who was arrested and charged in the lynching. It is ironic that he sat in a county commissioner's meeting and offered with the other commissioners what amounted to a reward for himself and other participants in the lynching. Who knows how many other commissioners were in attendance that night? He might well not have been the only one!

Lucy A. Oaks, wife of Isaac C. Oaks, rests in Lawrence Chapel Cemetery. She lived 23 Feb 1848/24 Jan 1890. *Note that she died before the lynching.* Isaac was born in 1846. He might well be buried in Lawrence Chapel also, but if so, it is under an unmarked stone. He was one of the three Justices of the Peace who presided at the inquest over the bodies of the Evanses on 16 Aug 1891.

On 21 Aug 1890 Isaac also married Mary J. Keller, in Cullman County. They quite possibly might be buried together in some other location. Was this a relative of Dr. Keller? She was about the right age to be a sister. I.C. Oaks also served as a bondsman for some of those charged.

John W. Goodlett, 23 Feb 1850/9 Sep 1908, a son of Bill "Billy" Goodlett, rests in Etha Cemetery. Bill and family once lived next door to Dr.. Keller and family in the vicinity of Old Enon Cemetery, and his daughter Eva, who married Mitchell, was named by Dr. Keller on the day that he delivered her, and the same day the village of Eva was named with the same name, since they had started out on the same day!

Little else is known about Bill Goodlett, except that he was one of those indicted but not brought to trial in the White Cap case.

Ben Goodlett ran a small country store at the intersection of the road running East from the old

Della Creel Store toward Welcome Church, and the road turning of South, going toward the Donaldson Bottoms, home of the Donaldson family.

M.B. "Ben" Goodlett , 18 May 1857/29 May 1924, brother to John, son to Billy, rests at Etha Cemetery also.

Both Arco Ray and Martha (Holcomb) Davis remember going to his store when they were children. Martha remembers him dressed in bib overalls, with a protruding paunch. Arco remembers him as a small man fitting Martha's description.

I have been able to learn nothing about the bad blood or feud between the Goodlett brothers and the Evanses, but a story is told of one of the Goodlett brothers dying in abject terror as he recalled the lynching in his last moments, screaming "Help me! They're coming after me with pitchforks"!

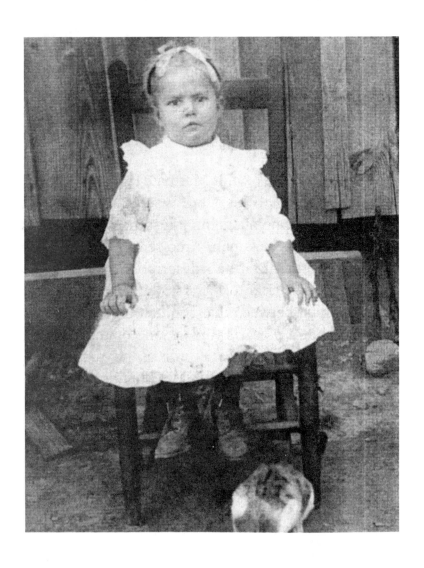

Martha Belle (Holcomb) Davis, born in 1905, has been a source of much inspiration, as well as information and help in my work on this book. Should I have looked around for a more up-to-date picture? I don't think so, as I simply love this one. It was made in about 1910. Thanks a million, Martha! (Sorry, but I don't know the cat's name!)

The Cast
Part four

Jim Cottle, one of those charged and tried, was James Madison Cottle, who lived 7 Dec 1854/25 Oct 1925. He married Dollie Ruth (?) and they rest at Pleasant Grove Cemetery. Also, Cullman County marriage records show that on 15 Sep 1897 James M. Cottle married Mary E. Lee. This is apparently another wife, but nothing else is known about her.

One bondsman for Jim Cottle was Fred N. Henderson, who on 17 Mar 1889 married Ella V. Guess, who was a sister to Aranna Guess, who married A.M.B. "Anse" Holmes. Anse was a brother to John S. Holmes and James Huston Holmes, as well as to my grandfather, Benjamin Franklin Holmes. This per Mabel (Holmes) Burks, daughter of Anse and Aranna.

Regrettably Mabel, a first cousin to my mother, passed away 12 Dec 1996 at the age of ninety three. She was a lovely lady!

Dr. G.W. McClarty's wife Sallie A. McClarty is buried in Pleasant Grove Cemetery, but if Dr. G.W. is buried there, then it is under an unmarked stone. She lived 25 May 1860/27 Dec 1900. Dr. McClarty also served as bondsman for defendants in the case.

The Doctor, in addition to being examining physician at the *post mortem* inquest was also one of those who reported seeing the blast and fire that destroyed or heavily damaged the Cullman County Court House in 1912, seeing it from Joppa, some fifteen or sixteen miles away!

That blast was a mystery to me, causing me to wonder what might be found in a court house before the use of natural gas, butane or propane for heat that could explode in such a violent manner, until I learned that the court house was where Cullman County stored it's dynamite for road construction until that time. I guess we can safely assume that practice was discontinued after that!

One of the mysteries confronting me without explanation is the brother of Dr. Keller, who was called "Joseph" in just about all newspaper accounts where he was mentioned, and was called "Josiah" in all hand written Court records. There is no doubt that it is the same person!

He apparently suffered an illness during the trial, as he was missing from the trial some of the time without explanation. This is speculation on my part.

I talked with Dr. Keller's daughter Ora (Keller) Holmes about that, and she simply remembered him as "Uncle Joe", which didn't shed any light on the situation, either.

I find him listed in Cullman County Marriages as Joseph P. Keller, marrying on 28 Oct 1877 a woman named Halda Elizabeth Smith. Ora had already told me he married "Hulda" something or other.

Bondsmen for Joseph, or Josiah Keller were G.W. McClarty, W.C. Winn, M.T. (Matthew) Self, and A.E. Drishel.

The E.W. Harper who was drawn as a juror, but did not sit on the case, was Elijah W. Harper, who lived at Walter, Alabama, where he was the first post master. The post office was named for his son Walter Harper.

Elijah Harper was also the author of the "Calf Ride" story appearing in Yesterday's Memories, reprinted from the Alabama Tribune, 1891.

John Humphrie, another way of spelling Humphrey, Humphries, etc. which represents one family line, and seem to have been used interchangeably by census takers and others, who was indicted and stood trial did on 24 Sep 1893 marry Nancy B. Huffstutler in Cullman County. John was a great uncle of Charles J. Humphries, who was very helpful in this research before his death in 1994, John was also a brother to Miles Humphries, brother in law to James Huston Holmes.

R.M. "Bob" Biggers, indicted but not tried, was Robert M. Biggers, who on 23 Dec 1891 married Emma H. Humphries. She was probably a sister to John, who stood trial in the lynching case, and Miles Humphries. This would have made him a brother in law to James Huston Holmes, as well.

He was a part of the same Biggers family as Carson "Carse" and Pierce Biggers. This Biggers family was quite prominent in the Cullman area, with Bob at one time running a mule barn, similar in many ways to a used car lot of today. Carse ran a livery stable in Cullman for years, and was also into banking, per Mabel (Holmes) Burks.

A.M. Nabors was a prominent figure in this whole scenario, giving us just about the *only* early information available other than census, or statistical information, on both William Monroe Evans and John W. Dickey. Unfortunately, he might not have been that accurate, as I have found some pretty glaring errors in what he had to say, compared to what others had to say about the same incidents.

The following is picked up from old newspapers, some of it from the Alabama Tribune, some from the Guntersville Democrat, and some from the Enquirer, published in Hartselle, along with the marriage books of Morgan County for corroboration.

Newspaper dated 17 Jan 1889: Mr. Samuel Ward was united in the Holy Bonds of Matrimony to Miss Nannie Nabors at the residence of the bride's father, Mr. A.M.Nabors, near Blue Springs, on Sunday, January 6th.

Marriage book entry reads: Nannie W. Nabors to Samuel Ward, 6 Jan 1889, ceremony by J.E. Weaver, MG (D-553)

Newspaper dated 25 Feb 1892: Robert D. Waldrop and Miss Laura Nabors were united in marriage today at the residence of the bride's father, A.M. Nabors, near Blue Springs.

Marriage book entry reads: Laura Nabors to Robert D. Waldrop 25 Feb 1892. Ceremony by E. (most likely Elijah) Ryan, JP (E-265)

Paper dated 15 Sep 1887: Died near Blue Springs August 26th, 1887, of congestive chill, Edward Harrison Nabors, son of A.M. and Eliza J. Nabors, aged 4 yr. 5 months and 28 days.

There is no available record of their burial site,

nor the family of A.M. and Eliza. It is likely Blue Springs, but there are many old unmarked graves there, as it is a rather old cemetery.

The preceding material was also covered in part by "Bits and Pieces", published by the Morgan County Genealogical Society.

Pierce Mooney, who was shot by John Henry Evans circa May, 1891, had as parents Martin H. "Boze" Mooney and Elizabeth M. (Jackson) Mooney, who were married on December 8, 1836, ceremony by Thomas Jones, Minister of the Gospel. (A-308)

"Boze" Mooney was the one abducted from his home and taken to the vicinity of Ryan's Cross Roads, seated against a tree, and shot to death. This was done by the notorious "Home Guards", who were largely baseless itinerants claiming to be guarding the homes of those away in the Confederate army fighting for "the cause". They robbed widows and orphans without qualm, sapping their life's blood without compunction.

Boze Mooney's body wasn't found for about two weeks, and he was interred on the site where he was found. This information per his great-nephew Henry Mooney.

Pierce Mooney on 19 Sep 1872 was married to Mary M. Evans, whom I believe to be a half-sister to William Monroe Evans. The marriage was performed by Thomas J Simpson, JP, at the residence of Joseph Yielding. Groom's permission signed by "X" Elizabeth Mooney. In the absence of Pierce

Mooney's picture, I will include one of his only son, William Franklin Mooney, and his bride Cloey (Fortner), taken about 1906, in Stigler, Oklahoma. It is here through the courtesy of Norene Dearmore, great granddaughter of Pierce Mooney, currently living in Lewisville, Tx.

Pierce is believed to have lived in the same area of Indian Territory as his son and daughter-in-law.

Pierce went there as soon as he healed after the shooting by the Evanses, and settled in the Indian Territory, where he lived out the rest of his life.

William Franklin, only son of Pierce Mooney and Mary M. (Evans) Mooney, with his bride of some twenty years. Picture made at Stigler, Oklahoma in 1906.

The Cast
Part five

I have been told in interviews that the man who tied the rope on the necks of William Monroe and John Henry Evans was Joseph "Joe" Gober , one of those who stood trial.

I find that impossible to either confirm or refute by any kind of documentation, but I'm sure someone did it, and it might well have been him. He was a tough man, known as a fighter.

W.G. Holmes, a bondsman, was Wiley Geneas Holmes, who married Marjorie Missouri Keller, a sister to Dr. L.M. Keller and Josiah, or Joseph Keller. W.G. was a son of William Carroll Holmes, and the father of Judson Pinkney Holmes, who was the father of Elna (Holmes) Graham, who married Elmer "Poss" Graham.

Poss was the driver of a school bus I rode as a lad while attending school at Eva, Alabama. Elna and Poss have a son named Virgil Graham, who currently operates a quail farm on part of the old Wiley Holmes farm. I can personally remember Wiley Holmes when I was a boy of about eleven. He was quite elderly at the time, circa 1943.

G.W. Peck was the Dr. Peck who built the "Peck Mansion" at Fort Bluff. He was the "Patron" doctor under whom Dr. L.M. Keller worked during his equivalent to an apprenticeship, or internship as it is used for training graduate doctors today. Dr. Peck was also a bondsman in this case.

181

A personal note pertaining to Dr. Peck comes to me from Noel Hardin:

It seems that Dr. Peck had been treating a hypochondriac lady for some time, and she showed signs of becoming a career patient. He was beginning to tire of hearing her complain when one day he was watering his horse from a road ditch when he saw some pretty white clay in the seams of the rock in the road bank. He dug out a wad of it, and was absent mindedly playing with it and manipulating it in his hands when he rolled a small piece of it into pill form.

This gave him an idea, and he rolled the rest of the wad into little ball, or 'pill" shapes, too. Next time he saw the lady he said "I have some pills that will either cure you or kill you". After the briefest hesitation she replied "I believe I'll chance it!" That was the last time he ever treated her, although she lived a healthy life for many years afterwards.

The Cast
Part six

D.W. Draper was at one time post master at Lawrence's Cove post office, as well as a bondsman in this case. He was a prominent citizen of that community. I only recently knew there had ever been a post office at Lawrence's Cove.

The judge who occupied the bench during this trial was the Honorable H.C. Speake. I have encountered little more about him.

James Matthew Heaton, the Justice of the Peace who figured prominently in the episode at Baileyton, Alabama has family, or at least there are people by that name in the area today. He is almost surely the one who delivered the paperwork to the Marshall County Sheriff, and took custody of John Henry Evans upon his arrest by the sheriff, then brought him back to Baileyton for trial, the last visit for John to Baileyton!

Heaton was also a signer of the petition for the creation of the Masonic Lodge #472 in Baileyton, along with Thomas M. Entrekin. Heaton became it's first Master.

William Cofer (W.T.L. Cofer) was a noted attorney in Cullman, Alabama, for some time. He was a defending attorney in the lynching trial for the murder of John Henry Evans, later becoming a Circuit Judge there.

Jesse Brown was also a defending attorney for those accused of the murder of John Henry Evans.

Ora (Keller) Holmes attended school at Eva in the sixth grade taught by Mrs. Jesse Brown, his wife, when the school stood on it's original location on Gravel Ridge, just North of Eva.

In March, 1905, Attorney Jesse B. Brown and Senator I.M. Hipp asked the City of Cullman for a telephone franchise. It caused a furor of protest, and less than a month later I.M. Hipp was assassinated near Joppa, Alabama.

Leonidas Cicero Dickey was the "Hired Gun", so to speak, on the defense team. He was a highly noted attorney who for a while worked with a law firm in Birmingham, Alabama. It seems somehow ironic that one of the team defending the lynch mob would share a surname with Mun Evans' former employer, John W. Dickey.

The three defense attorneys were the namesakes for William Leonidas Brown Keller, the son of Dr. Louis M. Keller that was born later in 1895, after the trial and acquittal of all defendants. This was no doubt an expression of appreciation by Dr. Keller for the able job they did in the group's defense!

This was told to me by Dr. Keller's youngest daughter, Ora (Keller) Holmes, wife of Archie Bethel Holmes.

My research also led me to a great grandson of William Monroe Evans, named Norris Evans. He resides in Atalla, Alabama. His grandfather was George Evans, eleven years younger than John Henry Evans. His father was Robert Lee Evans. Pictures of Norris and his wife Bobbie, along with

Joan Mims (artist who drew the cover of this book), who is both an Evans and Bradford relative.

We had the pleasure of spending a day together looking at all of the pertinent locations involved in the lynching, and I was very happy to become acquainted with them! It was also a pleasure to introduce them to my cherished friend Margaret Jean Jones!

Willis C. Stephens was the one who led the posse in the pursuit that ended in the confrontation at Wild Goat Cove. He was a son of Nicholas Stephens, and a brother to Mary Polly (Stephens) Evans, wife or consort of William Monroe Evans. He spent about one year in the John W. Dickey scout company, in the company of "Mun" Evans, among others, then after the dissolution of the company he worked on rebuilding the Memphis and Charleston Railroad until the end of the war. Then he apparently became a deputy sheriff, and was leader of the posse in that episode known as the "shoot-out" at Wild Goat Cove.

Willis C. Stephens was not involved in, nor aware of, the Evans lynching, as far as I can determine. He left Alabama for Texas in January of 1895, while coincidentally the lynching trial was being readied for the court. There he became a Medical Doctor, serving in that capacity for many years, and his son followed in his footsteps in that calling.

The latter portion of this information is through the courtesy of Don and Nelda Kirk, descendants of Willis C. Stephens.

185

Mary Polly (Stephens) Evans, the sixth child of Nicholas Stephens, was not to be envied for her part in this scenario! The stories of the beginning of her association with Mun Evans are many, but most are of very questionable credibility. They range all of the way from actual kidnapping from the Stephens home at gun point to voluntary marriage, of which I have found no record. There is the possibility that the marriage records might have perished at the hands of Union troops during the Civil War, as they destroyed many documents wantonly and willfully, but since this confrontation and related events didn't occur until 1869, and the Civil War ended in 1865, this is rather unlikely. This marriage was very closely associated with the affair at Wild Goat Cove, which occurred in 1869.

This was all part of the disguised persons taking the shotgun from the home of Nicholas Stephens, involving or as a result of William Monroe Evans' seduction of Stephens' daughter.

Charles Humphries told me of a time when he was visiting, as a lad, the Fletcher Allen family, who lived in the old Evans house, where the Evans family lived at the time of the lynching, when two ladies, one quite elderly, and the other middle aged, came to the Allen residence and asked if they could look through the house. Permission granted, they walked slowly through the house, mentioning tearfully to each other how certain things "used to be". The indications are that these were Mary Polly Evans and one of her daughters, either Molly or Milona, but the identity is not confirmed.

It must have been very difficult for her to ignore the depredations and shenanigans of her spouse, or mate of several years, while she tried to raise his children. I am personally thinking that her social life must have been practically nonexistent!

I am totally unaware of the location and circumstances of her later life and death, such as where she and other family members lived and died after the death of William Monroe and John Henry Evans. Of all people involved in this entire situation, her lot was quite probably the least desirable or enviable!

I have also talked with a granddaughter of William Monroe Evans, descended from his son Joe Evans. He is the elusive one, of whom I have heard a little bit, and heard it a lot of times. He had a club or deformed foot, and married Sallie Campbell.

Julius Damus was elected Mayor of Cullman, Alabama in 1879. Shortly afterwards he entered the race for Circuit Clerk. He lost the race, but after some horse-trading he wound up with the office!

Andrew J. York, Sheriff, was a former Cullman City councilman and city marshal. He also arrested William Monroe Evans on a warrant for carrying a concealed weapon on his person. He was the foreman of the grand jury indicting the White Caps for the lynching of the Evanses, too. The order in which he held these positions is not clear.

SUSPENDED SENTENCE
Epilogue

The old hickory tree that held the grisly burden that night stayed around until the 1940's before finally succumbing to decay and gravity. It was there in my lifetime, although dead. One of the strange quirks of fate is that the limb that supported those two bodies was the last to go! It was almost as if it stayed around longer than the other branches to apologize for the service it performed that night! It has been more than a century since the famous, or infamous, depending upon the point of view, night of August 15th, 1891. All of those who participated in the affair, whether as "hangors" or "hangees" are gone, and in many cases apparently forgotten, as some of them seem to have disappeared from the face of the earth.

It is understandable why some of them would have dropped several points in popularity with their neighbors by turning State's evidence against their fellow participants to save their own skins, inclining them to seek solitude and anonymity away from the community where the event occurred.

Then on the other hand, one might also understand how it would feel to believe in your little "heart of hearts" that you had one possible way to avoid leaving your wife and children forever, and that was to rat on your friends. That would be a burden that not many of us could carry very well, or at least any better than they did!

It was obvious from the start that the prosecution was willing to pay any price within it's reach to convict the leadership of the mob, even to the extent of releasing people as guilty as those who stood trial for the sake of a conviction. They were obviously not aware that a very substantial percentage of the citizenry wanted William Monroe and John Henry Evans dead, as they were an imminent threat to the law-abiding residents of the country, and the duly constituted law and authority had proven itself either unwilling or unable to cope with the situation. Protection from the likes of that pair was a right the people of the community considered theirs, and it was not provided by the "powers that be", leading them to believe that if they wanted relief it must come from their own hands.

Had they calmly led them out and shot them in a quiet manner, especially privately, away from the hands of the law, it would have created only a fraction of the clamor for "justice" that the hanging did. The whole investigation and prosecution were probably the biggest for the longest period of time that the State of Alabama has ever known! It was conducted extensively for over three years before an arrest was made! However, I find it difficult to believe, but there wasn't any investigative newspaper reporting done whatsoever that I can find, nor were there front page headlines. It wasn't their style of the day!

The size of the mob was estimated at from 25 to 200 persons, and frankly at this time I have no idea

189

of the number, although I am convinced it must have fallen between those two numbers. In my research, I have dealt with at least as many as the lower number, and I have no reason to believe I ever considered them all!

There were two waves of convictions they hoped to obtain, one being the primary, or leadership group, such as the eight who were actually tried, along with another group to follow, such as John Holmes, Bill Goodlett, and Bob Biggers, who would have been part of the next trial, had the first one been successful. Then there would have probably been another wave of indictments!

When the first one failed, the rest were abandoned, as the State then saw that it was hopeless to try for a conviction. The first trial was for the hanging of John H. Evans, with the State thinking he was the softer touch for a conviction, with sympathy for his tender age, but he was probably hated even more than his father. He definitely had a psychopathic personality, with the conscience of a snake!

After the failure of the first trial, the other trial or trials never occurred. The prosecution "overlooked one little detail" as the detective writers tell us in all of the "Whodunits", and that is what had to be the solemn truth, that they couldn't impanel a jury of twelve people in Cullman County who would convict those charged, regardless of proof. It is pretty easy to see that the defendants did just about precisely what they were charged with, but the jury still didn't consider them guilty!

One of the things I learned from the daughter of Dr. L.M. Keller is that Dr. Keller had a son, born in 1895, the year of the trial, named William Leonidas Brown Keller. My mother and her siblings were personally acquainted with Brown Keller.

He was named for W.T.L. (William) Cofer, Leonidas Cicero Dickey, (Leonidas) and Jesse Brown (Brown), the three defense attorneys who so ably defended those accused. This is no doubt a measure of the gratitude and relief felt by Dr. Keller, as well as those others who were exonerated by the court at that time.

Dr. Keller's daughter, Ora (Keller) Holmes, although only twelve years old when Dr. Keller died in 1909, told me that her mother would answer anything she chose to ask about this affair openly and frankly, but with no elaboration whatsoever! She said that while Dr. Keller was in jail it was almost like an "Open Door" policy, with him continuing to practice medicine and treat patients, even though he was theoretically locked up.

Most of the reason for that was that the local officialdom knew that these were all substantial citizens, with property and family, who wouldn't be leaving anyway, so they were quite lenient with them while they were confined. They might have even been looking forward to future elections, knowing the influence those charged had excercised in the area, and very well might again!

This kind of puts the "kibosh" on Uncle John Holmes' story about the jail time in Hartselle, told to

Mabel (Holmes) Burks, as there was no confirming documentation that I could find!

So many stories were told to so many different people that the truth, and for that matter, reason, doesn't seem to fit in with any of the stories told then. However, they did have a lot of incentive to create false stories for family and friends.

The prosecuting attorneys, or "solicitors" went on to become fixtures in Cullman County politics for many years yet to come, in some cases. The name "St. John" is still with us in Cullman today, as I read just a few years ago where Finis St. John IV perished in a tractor accident involving fire ants. He is a direct descendant of the St. John involved in prosecuting this case.

Many of the names mentioned as "participants" will be familiar to many people as "grandpa", or "great grandpa", as a lot of them still have descendants living in the area, many of whom never heard of the lynching at Baileyton on that night of August 15th, 1891. The cover-up was a good one!

It is not my intent to disturb the long-dead, but to "Let sleeping dogs lie" is to ignore reality, the history of which is to this day a strong integral part of our lives, causing many people to be born other than where they would have been had not the lynching made migration necessary for many people, and with said history being born when the mob gave William Monroe "Mun" Evans and his son John Henry Evans, a **"SUSPENDED SENTENCE"**!